MW01612812

Learning Basic Social Skills

Nancy Lobb

illustrated by Jennifer DeCristoforo

User's Guide
to
Walch Reproducible Books

As part of our general effort to provide educational materials that are as practical and economical as possible, we have designated this publication a "reproducible book." The designation means that purchase of the book includes purchase of the right to limited reproduction of all pages on which this symbol appears:

Here is the basic Walch policy: We grant to individual purchasers of this book the right to make sufficient copies of reproducible pages for use by all students of a single teacher. This permission is limited to a single teacher and does not apply to entire schools or school systems, so institutions purchasing the book should pass the permission on to a single teacher. Copying of the book or its parts for resale is prohibited.

Any questions regarding this policy or requests to purchase further reproduction rights should be addressed to:

Permissions Editor
J. Weston Walch, Publisher
321 Valley Street • P. O. Box 658
Portland, Maine 04104-0658

1   2   3   4   5   6   7   8   9   10

ISBN 0-8251-3885-X

Contents ....

Unit III Getting Along with Others

Unit IV Developing Conversation Skills

Unit V Having a Good Work Attitude

To the Teacher ....

Learning Basic Social Skills is written for students with special needs. Its purpose is to teach the social skills needed to succeed in daily living and on the job.

While all teachers of special students recognize the importance of teaching social skills to their students, these skills may be among the most difficult for the classroom teacher to teach. *Learning Basic Social Skills* will give teachers of special students materials and methods to help their students gain competence socially, a prerequisite to success on the job and in everyday life.

The goal of *Learning Basic Social Skills* is to break down complex social skills into easily understood components. Research has shown consistently that the overwhelming reason special students may not succeed socially or on the job is not the quality of their work. Most often it is their unacceptable appearance, behavior, and attitudes. While most of us acquire social skills through observing others, many special students cannot discern these rules on their own. Thus, the need arises for special teaching of basic social rules. *Learning Basic Social Skills* presents these rules in a variety of ways, emphasizing learning through role-playing and cooperative learning activities.

Learning Basic Social Skills is a reproducible teacher book containing both teacher sections and student sections. Each teacher section includes objectives, vocabulary, and numerous additional activities pertaining to the student material that follows it. The answer key for all sections may be found on page 91.

Reproducible student pages are identified by the copyright line with a flame logo at the bottom. They can be copied and distributed to each student.

Student sections contain very short reading sections written on a third grade reading level. They are followed by several activities in which the student is asked to think about and apply the information given in the reading.

Also included are reproducible pages marked "Student Journal Page." These pages give students a way to think about their own social skill levels in a more private format. These pages are meant to be reproduced and distributed to students. However, these pages can be filled out and kept by the student, not graded by the teacher. They may be stapled together to form a journal which the student can keep and refer to. Their purpose is to facilitate a private forum for introspection by the student. As such, these pages would not necessarily be shared with the class or even seen by the teacher, although the teacher may require that the students complete the work.

UNIT 1
Looking Your Best

UNIT I
Looking Your Best . . . .

Objectives

Students will understand the importance of good grooming. Students will know what to do to be well-groomed.

Vocabulary

antiperspirant	dandruff	fluoride	interview
appearance	deodorant	grooming	odor
application	emery board	hair stylist	scent
appointment	employer	hangnail	
cuticle	floss	infection	

Additional Activities

1. Discuss why good grooming is important in making and keeping friends, in dating, and at work.

2. Invite a hair stylist to visit the class. The stylist could talk about shampoos and conditioners and how best to wash the hair. The stylist could also talk about choosing a flattering hairstyle.

3. Invite a dentist or hygienist to speak to the class about proper oral hygiene. He or she might discuss how to choose and use a toothbrush, or describe what happens at a checkup.

4. Discuss the prevention of foot odor. Students may not realize that there are different types of socks available. Cotton socks tend to absorb moisture and eliminate some foot odor. Nylon or polyester socks may aggravate moisture and odor problems.

5. Invite a makeup specialist to speak to the women of the class on the proper use of makeup for various occasions.

6. Invite a manicurist to discuss proper care of the nails. Have nail clippers, emery boards, and nail files available. Have students practice proper nail-trimming techniques. Polish could also be available for class members who wish to practice applying it.

7. Have a dermatologist or nurse speak to the class about proper care of the skin to prevent oily skin, pimples, blackheads, and acne. The importance of a good diet to healthy skin should be discussed, along with foods that aggravate skin conditions. The variety of skin-care products available at a drugstore could also be discussed.

8. Hold a private session for the women of the class to discuss feminine hygiene. This discussion should include personal hygiene, use of feminine hygiene products, and such.

9. Hold a concurrent session for the men of the class to discuss special male grooming problems such as body odor, shaving, trimming of facial hair, and foot odor.

10. Divide the students into pairs. Each pair should present a short, humorous skit showing a consequence of poor grooming. For example:

    (a) A girl and boy on a date are sitting closer and closer together. Then she gets a whiff of his breath. She starts moving the other way.

    (b) A hairdresser begins work on a customer. The hairdresser's body odor quickly convinces the customer not to make a return visit.

11. Discuss and demonstrate proper posture. Have each student evaluate his or her sitting and standing posture. Discuss how good posture can improve one's appearance.

The Importance of Good Grooming

Oscar and Miguel were looking for part-time jobs. They saw an ad in the newspaper. They both called to set up job interviews.

Oscar went to his interview straight from track practice. He was sweaty and his hair wasn't combed. Oscar was wearing shorts and a T-shirt. He had on dirty tennis shoes and no socks.

The interviewer asked Oscar a few questions. Then she gave Oscar an application to fill out. As Oscar worked, he chewed loudly on a piece of grape gum.

Miguel had his interview next. He had left track practice early so he could go home and shower. He dressed in a clean shirt and slacks. His shoes were polished.

The interviewer asked Miguel the same questions she had asked Oscar. Then she gave Miguel the job application to fill out. Miguel worked quietly and neatly.

The interviewer quickly decided who would get the job. The answer was easy. Oscar's poor grooming cost him the job.

It may not seem fair, but other people do judge us by how we look. Most employers feel strongly about the appearance of their workers. Poor grooming is a big reason people are turned down for jobs.

• • *What Do You Think?*

1. Many employers feel that a well-groomed person will do better work on the job. Why do you think employers feel this way?

   _____

   _____

2. What do you think a person's grooming (or lack of it) tells others?

   _____

   _____

Clean Up Your Act!

Have you ever watched old cowboy movies? Every Saturday night the cowboys rode into town after a long week of riding the range.

They would head for the bathhouse and plunk down their two bits (a quarter). This would buy a tub of warm water for their weekly bath "whether they needed it or not." You can be sure these fellows needed it long before bath time!

It's easier to come by hot water these days. So, there is really no excuse for having body odor.

Taking a bath or shower every day is the way to start. Plain old soap and water will wash off dirt, germs, and sweat.

Put on clean underwear and socks every day.

Next, use a deodorant or antiperspirant. Deodorants control body odor. Antiperspirants control odor and keep your underarms dry. But, neither takes the place of that daily washing.

If you use a scent (such as perfume, cologne, or aftershave), use only a little. Strong scents may bother other people. Again, these products do not take the place of washing. They do not wash away dirt, germs, and sweat. These products only hide odors.

If you do all these things daily, you'll be clean—and you'll smell great!

(continued)

Clean Up Your Act! *(continued)*

• • *What Did You Learn?*

1. How do you remove dirt, germs, and sweat from your skin?

   _____

   _____

   _____

2. How are deodorants and antiperspirants different?

   _____

   _____

   _____

3. Why don't scents take the place of daily washing?

   _____

   _____

   _____

4. What two pieces of clothing should always be changed daily?

   _____

   _____

   _____

Your Crowning Glory

Have you ever had a "bad hair day"? That's a day you feel like wearing a hat to hide your hair.

Everyone has hair troubles from time to time. Magazines are full of articles about hair care. Many products promise beautiful, shiny hair.

For you to be well-groomed, your hair should look its best. It should be clean and neatly cut. The style should look good on you.

The hard part is that hair care is not the same for everyone. What works well for one person may not work for another. A person with thick, curly hair needs different hair care than a person with fine, thin hair. The same style looks good on one person and not so good on someone else.

So, what is the answer? How can you learn what works on your head of hair? A good way to start is to find a hair stylist you like. Do you have a friend whose hair looks nice? Ask this friend who works on his or her hair.

When you find a stylist you like, work together to find a style that is easy to care for and suits your face.

No matter what type of hair you have, you must keep it clean. Wash it as often as needed, even every day. Try different shampoos until you find one that leaves your hair looking good.

There are shampoos for dry, oily, and normal hair. If you have trouble with dandruff, choose a dandruff shampoo. Shampoo as often as you need to, to keep your hair looking clean and free from dandruff and oil.

By keeping your hair clean and neatly cut, you will add a lot to your looks! If your hair is dirty or has flakes, you will not look good—no matter how well-dressed you are.

•• *What Did You Learn?*

1. How can a good hair stylist help you?

_____

2. How can you choose a shampoo?

_____

Name_____ Date _____

Be Handy with Hand Care

Imagine you are trying out a new restaurant. The person who waits on you has dirty hands and broken, dirty fingernails. Would you still want to eat there? A person with poorly groomed hands will not last long in the food business!

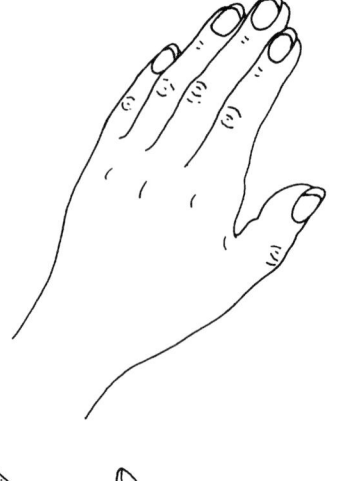

Clean hands and well-shaped nails are important to looking well-groomed. Soap and water can take care of most dirt. A nailbrush can help get out any dirt from under your nails.

As you dry your hands after washing, gently push back your cuticles with the towel. Do not clip your cuticles. That will make them rough. It also increases the risk of hangnails or infection.

Use nail clippers to trim your nails. First, cut them straight across. Then, round the corners to the shape you want. An emery board or a nail file can smooth and shape your nails.

If you use nail polish, apply it neatly. When the polish begins to chip, remove it right away. It is better to wear no polish than to wear chipped polish.

• • What Did You Learn?

1. How can you get dirt out from under your fingernails?

_____

2. Why shouldn't you clip your cuticles?

_____

3. What three tools can be used to trim and shape the nails?

_____

4. What is the best way to push back your cuticles?

_____

Face the Facts

An attractive smile adds a lot to your looks! But, dirty teeth or bad breath can quickly turn people off. Luckily, it is not hard to take care of your teeth.

Brush your teeth at least twice a day (morning and night). Use a fluoride toothpaste. Fluoride toothpaste has been proven to help prevent tooth decay. Ask your dentist what type of toothbrush you should use.

After brushing, use dental floss between all your teeth. Floss gets out pieces of food your brush can't reach.

Keeping your teeth clean will prevent cavities and gum disease. It will also help keep your breath smelling fresh.

Visit your dentist regularly. This way, you can take care of any problems while they are still small.

Another area of grooming is just for women. Those who wear makeup need to learn how to apply it right. Using too much makeup is not attractive. Clerks at the department store or pharmacy makeup counter can show you how to apply makeup at no cost.

Finally, a word for the men. If you decide to grow a beard or mustache, keep it trimmed to stay neat. Use shampoo to wash it whenever you wash your hair.

•• *What Did You Learn?*

1. What kind of toothpaste should you buy?

   _____

   _____

2. What is the purpose of dental floss?

   _____

   _____

   _____

(continued)

Face the Facts *(continued)*

3. Why should you visit the dentist regularly?

_____

_____

_____

_____

4. Where could a person learn how to use makeup?

_____

_____

_____

5. How often a day should you brush your teeth?

_____

_____

_____

Name_____ Date _____

A Grooming Timetable

Directions: How often do you think you need to do each task below to keep looking your best? Beside each task, write **daily, twice a day, weekly,** and so on. (Not everyone will have the same answers.)

Task	How Often?
1. Brush your teeth	
2. Floss your teeth	
3. See your dentist for a checkup	
4. Change underwear and socks	
5. Change shirt or blouse	
6. Brush or comb your hair	
7. Wash your hands	
8. Trim your nails	
9. Take a bath or shower	
10. Use deodorant or antiperspirant	
11. Get a haircut	
12. Wash your face	
13. Use cologne or aftershave	
14. Wash your hair	
15. Use a nailbrush	
16. (Women) Put on makeup	
17. (Women) Put on nail polish	
18. (Men) Trim beard or mustache	
19. (Men) Shave	
20. Check your appearance in a mirror	

Name_____ Date _____

Unit Test

Directions: Fill in the blanks below with the correct words from the box.

shower	appearance
dentist	shampoo
trimming	deodorants
fluoride	floss
emery board	soap
bath	

1. To keep clean, take a _____ or _____ daily.

2. _____ is a product that removes dirt and germs from the skin.

3. Products that help prevent body odor are antiperspirants and _____ .

4. Try different kinds of _____ to see which makes your hair look the best.

5. Use a nail file or an _____ to smooth and shape your nails.

6. To prevent problems with your teeth and gums, visit your _____ regularly.

7. A mustache or beard needs regular _____ .

8. Always buy _____ toothpaste.

9. _____ cleans the spaces between your teeth.

10. Your _____ tells others a lot about you.

(continued)

Unit Test *(continued)*

•• *What Do You Think?*

11. How do you think good grooming can help you get along better with other people?

_____

_____

_____

_____

12. Why do you think good grooming can help you feel good about yourself?

_____

_____

_____

_____

Name_____ Date _____

A Grooming Checklist

Directions: Think about your grooming during the last 24 hours. Mark an **X** under **Yes** or **No** for each item listed below.

	YES	NO
1. I took a bath or shower in the last 24 hours.		
2. I used a deodorant today.		
3. My hair is neat, clean, and well-cut.		
4. My face and hands are clean.		
5. My fingernails are clean and trimmed.		
6. I brushed and flossed my teeth last night.		
7. I brushed my teeth this morning.		
8. My clothes are neat and clean.		
9. I put on clean underwear and socks today.		
10. I used only a little (or no) cologne or aftershave today.		
11. I washed my face this morning.		
12. My shoes are clean and/or polished.		
13. I used only a little (or no) makeup today.		
14. My nail polish is not chipped, or I am not wearing nail polish.		
15. I shaved if needed, or I keep my beard or mustache trimmed and clean.		
16. I checked my appearance in a mirror before I left the house today.		
17. I like the way I look today.		

Name_____ Date_____

My Grooming Plan

Directions: Use the grooming checklist on page 14 to make lists of your strong and weak points in grooming in the spaces below. Under the areas that need work, write your plan for improvement.

My grooming strong points are: _____

_____

_____

_____

_____

My grooming weak points are:_____

_____

_____

_____

_____

I could improve my weak points by: _____

_____

_____

_____

_____

UNIT II
Choosing and Caring for Clothes

UNIT II
Choosing and Caring for Clothes....................

Objective

Students will understand the importance of wearing clean, unwrinkled, appropriate clothing.

Vocabulary

casual	inexpensive	preshrunk	rayon
dry clean	occasion	quality	trendy
fabric	polyester		

Additional Activities

1. Have students bring in newspaper ads or magazines showing the latest clothing styles. Ask students to choose some styles they like. Discuss the positive and negative aspects of the different styles. In what situations would each style be appropriate (sports, dressy occasion, work, school, etc.)?

2. Have students cut out a picture of clothing that would be appropriate for: school, an office job, casual wear, and party wear. Students should glue each picture to a piece of paper. Under each picture, they should explain why that clothing would look good on them and be suitable for the occasion.

3. Discuss principles for choosing clothing that is comfortable and flattering. For example, a heavy person might want to accentuate his or her height by wearing horizontal stripes. A short person could wear narrow vertical stripes or outfits of one color to appear taller.

4. Have students find out which colors of clothing might be most flattering to them. If possible, obtain a variety of color swatches and let students work

with these by holding them up and looking in the mirror to see what looks best. Many books and articles have been written on "choosing your colors."

5. Discuss appropriate types of clothing for various situations. For example: a wedding, a party, a school dance, a job interview, or on the job.

6. Discuss ways to make money go farther when buying clothing. Some ideas are:

    • Buying clothing that will mix and match. By sticking to a color scheme, your clothes will go together, making more outfits possible from fewer articles of clothing.

    • Finding good quality clothing at garage sales, resale or thrift shops.

    • Buying clothing of lesser known or store brands (as opposed to designer clothing).

    • Shopping sales wisely. Learn when clearance sales are held (usually at the end of the season). Read clothing ads in the newspaper.

7. Discuss how to tell if clothing is well made. Bring in examples of shirts that are well made or poorly made. (You might obtain some poorly made shirts from a thrift shop.) Students should learn to look for:

    • smooth, even seams

    • neatly finished buttonholes (no loose threads)

    • flat, even hems

    • patterns or plaids that match at the seams

    • buttons that are sewn on well

    • a fabric that will be easy to care for (This can be determined by reading the label for fabric content. Also, students can examine the fabric to see if it looks strong.)

8. Bring in clothing with various labels. Discuss how these items should be cared for.

9. Bring in a selection of laundry products (detergent, soap, stain removers, and bleach). Discuss how these products should be used for best results. Read the labels. Ask students questions about the directions and cautions on the labels. (For more practice reading labels, see *Reading Labels Activity Pack* by J. Weston Walch, Publisher.) Talk about which laundry products you would use on the sample clothing from activity 8.

10. Demonstrate a few basic mending techniques such as repairing a rip, sewing on a button, and repairing a hem that is coming out. Have materials available for each student to use for practice.

11. Discuss how to use a washing machine and dryer for best results. An instruction booklet from these appliances will give you some guidelines. Discuss how to line dry clothing.

12. Visit a laundromat. Demonstrate use of the washer and dryer. Discuss different washing and drying temperatures and how to sort clothing before washing.

13. Bring an iron, ironing board, and some old shirts to school. Demonstrate the proper way to iron a shirt. Have students practice doing this themselves.

14. Go to a clothing store. Have each student pick a shirt or blouse they like. Read the labels. Discuss the care that would be needed for each item chosen. How easy would it be to wash? Would it need dry cleaning? Would it require ironing? Does it look like it would last a long time? How would students rate the overall quality of the item?

15. Have students call or visit a dry cleaner to find out the price for cleaning some basic items of clothing: shirt, slacks, dress, suit, etc. Have these students share their findings with the class. (The purpose of this exercise is to make students aware of the extra cost associated with purchases that will need professional cleaning. Some items, such as a suitcoat, will always need dry cleaning. With other items, such as a woman's blouse, students should be aware that they will end up spending more if they choose a blouse that must be dry cleaned.)

16. Have students work in small groups to make posters showing care labels on different types of clothing. For example, one group might draw a white rayon blouse with a care label reading "dry clean only."

Dress for Success

"Clothes make the man (or woman)."
"Dress for success."

You may have heard these old sayings. They have been around a long time because they have a lot of truth in them.

How you dress does affect how others see you. This does not mean you need to have expensive clothes to look good. You need to know how to keep your clothes neat and clean. You need to learn to spend your clothing dollars wisely. And, you need to know how to choose clothes that are right for the occasion.

•• Keeping Your Clothes Neat and Clean

You will save yourself a lot of trouble by buying clothing that is easy to care for. How can you tell which clothes will be easy to take care of?

When you shop for clothing, read the label before you buy. The label will give care instructions. It may say "machine washable," "needs no ironing," or "dry clean only." It is important to follow these directions exactly. If you don't, you may ruin the piece of clothing.

The label will also tell you what type of fabric the clothing is made of. An article made of 100 percent cotton will wear well. But, it will probably need ironing. And, it may shrink unless the label says "preshrunk."

Clothes made of a cotton/polyester blend also wear well. They usually do not need ironing if they are dried at the right temperature and removed from the dryer before it stops. Don't stuff the dryer too full or all your clothes will be wrinkled. Clothes made of rayon or wool must usually be dry cleaned. This adds to the overall cost of the article.

So, read the label carefully. If you are not sure how easy the article will be to care for, ask a clerk. Questions to ask are: How well will this hold up? Can it be machine washed? Will it need ironing?

Choosing Easy-Care Clothing

André had started doing all his own laundry. He noticed right away that some of his clothes came out looking fine. Others shrank. Others were a mass of wrinkles.

André needed to buy some clothes before he started his new job. He wanted to be sure to pick out clothes that would come out of the dryer looking great. He did not want to have to iron. He did not want the clothes to shrink. And, he wanted to spend little to care for the clothes.

André went shopping. He looked at a variety of shirts. He chose three shirts he liked. Then he read the label on each shirt.

For each shirt, choose one reason it might be a good choice. Then, give one reason André might not want to buy that shirt.

1. Shirt A (100 percent cotton):

   This is a good choice because: _____

   A reason not to buy is: _____

2. Shirt B (65 percent cotton and 35 percent polyester):

   This is a good choice because: _____

   A reason not to buy is: _____

3. Shirt C (rayon shirt marked "Dry Clean Only"):

   This is a good choice because: _____

   A reason not to buy is: _____

Which shirt do you think André should buy? _____

Stretch Your Clothing Dollar

Nels had worked all summer on the road crew. He wanted to use some of his money for school clothes. He had outgrown his old clothes over the summer. He wondered how he could buy enough to wear without spending all of his money.

He asked three friends for advice. Here is what they said:

Carlos: "Buy a whole lot of the cheapest stuff you can find. Don't worry if it's well made. You need a lot of stuff."
Tawana: "Buy two pairs of good pants in basic colors. Then get a few good shirts that go with either pair."
Joy: "Buy one very expensive, but great-looking, outfit!"

Which friend do you think gave Nels the best advice? Why?

Let's see what Nels decided to do.

Nels decided to go with Tawana's advice. First, he looked in the newspaper. He found a store that was having a big sale.

He bought two pairs of pants. One was a pair of blue jeans. The other was a pair of tan pants. He chose several shirts of different styles. All of them would match either pair of pants. He also chose a sweater that would "dress up" the pants. By choosing two basic colors for his pants, Nels could "mix and match" his shirts and sweater to make more outfits.

All the items Nels chose were of good quality. Nels asked the clerk to help him be sure they would wash well and need no ironing. He wanted the clothes to look good all year.

What about Carlos's advice? Buying a lot of cheaply made clothes would give Nels lots to wear at first. But, clothes that are not well made will not last long. They won't look good very long either. If Nels had followed Carlos's advice, he would have had to replace the clothes sooner.

Joy's advice was not so good either. If Nels had bought just one expensive, but great-looking, outfit, he'd have to wear it every day. Chances are, he'd get pretty tired of it!

Most of us don't outgrow all our clothes each year. Still, we can learn from the "mix and match" lesson. By planning your clothes around a few basic colors and carefully choosing things that will fit into your overall plan, you'll get more for your money.

Name_____ Date _____

The Dryer Ate My Shirt!

Directions: Put an **X** beside each item that needs washing.

_____ 1. Underwear that has been worn one day.

_____ 2. A shirt that has been worn once. It doesn't look dirty, but it smells bad.

_____ 3. Washable slacks that have been worn twice. They smell O.K., but they are very wrinkled.

_____ 4. A shirt on which you spilled grape juice.

_____ 5. Socks that have been worn only one day.

_____ 6. A dirty coat marked "Dry Clean Only."

_____ 7. A dress that has been worn to a party. It looks and smells clean.

Directions: Read each label and the sentences beside it. Put an **X** beside each correct way to take care of the clothing.

_____ 8. Take the sweater to the dry cleaners.

_____ 9. Wash the sweater carefully by hand.

_____ 10. Machine wash the sweater in cold water.

_____ 11. Wash the pants in detergent and hot water.

_____ 12. Take the pants to be dry cleaned.

_____ 13. Wash the pants in warm water, then put them in the dryer.

_____ 14. Wash the pants in warm water, soap, and bleach.

_____ 15. Take the pants out of the dryer as soon as (or before) the cycle ends.

Dry Clean Only

Machine wash warm. Tumble dry. Remove promptly. Do not bleach.

24   *Learning Basic Social Skills*

The Right Clothes for the Occasion

• • *A Job Interview*

You have an interview for a job in a grocery store. You wonder what to wear. Circle the letter that shows the best choice:

  (a) clean jeans and a T-shirt

  (b) slacks, a dress shirt and tie (or a suit and tie) if you're a man; a dress or skirt and blouse if you're a woman

  (c) shorts (It is hot outside.)

(The best choice is B. It's best not to look too casual. The employer may think you're not serious about the job.)

• • *The First Day on a New Job*

You did well at your interview. You have been hired as a checker at the grocery store. You wonder what you should wear on your first day at work. Circle the letter of the best choice:

  (a) Dress up in your best clothes to make a good impression on everyone.

  (b) Wear anything you feel like so everyone will get to know the "real you."

  (c) Ask your boss what to wear when you are offered the job.

(The best choice is C. The store probably has rules for how its workers should dress. Find out what they expect of you. The store wants its employees to look good. Their appearance reflects on the store itself.)

• • *Party Clothes*

You celebrate your new job by having a party. You want something new and trendy to wear. This is something you probably will not wear many times. Circle the letter of the best choice:

  (a) The sky's the limit! After all, it is a party!

  (b) The finest quality at any price.

  (c) Something fun but not expensive.

(The best choice is C. You'll only wear this outfit a few times. So, it doesn't need to last a long time.)

Name_____ Date _____

I Don't Have a Thing to Wear!

Directions: Read the following descriptions of occasions. Then, write what you think each person below should wear. (There is more than one correct answer for each occasion.)

1. Evan is taking Maria to a movie. What do you think he should wear?	4. Kent is going to a funeral. What do you think he should wear?
2. Jamara is applying for a job as a waitress. What do you think she should wear? Should she use makeup?	5. Rita is starting work in an office. What do you think she should wear?
3. Sue and Omar are going to a big wedding. It will be a formal afternoon wedding. What do you think they should wear?	6. Juan is applying for a job at a gas station. He has an interview with the owner. What do you think he should wear?

How Would You Know?

Directions: Write the best answer to each of the following questions.

1. How would you know if a blouse or shirt you see on sale will wash well and not need ironing?

   _____

   _____

   _____

2. How would you know if you look your best before leaving for work or school?

   _____

   _____

3. How would you know what to wear to a party you've been invited to?

   _____

   _____

4. How would you know if a coat you're thinking of buying is well made?

   _____

   _____

   _____

5. How would you know if an item you've worn needs to be washed?

   _____

   _____

6. How would you know if a style or color looks good on you?

   _____

   _____

   _____

Unit Test

Directions: Write **True** or **False** beside each statement below. Discuss the correct answers as a class.

_____ 1. When you are hired for a job, ask your boss what you should wear to work.

_____ 2. If you are buying an item of clothing you will wear a lot, make sure it's of good quality.

_____ 3. To stretch your wardrobe, choose a few basic colors that you can mix and match.

_____ 4. You should not wash an item if the label says "Dry Clean Only."

_____ 5. A cotton/polyester blouse shouldn't need ironing.

_____ 6. It doesn't matter what you wear to work as long as it is clean.

_____ 7. Wear your best jeans to a job interview.

_____ 8. Clothes of 100 percent cotton may shrink when washed unless they are preshrunk.

_____ 9. How you dress affects how others think of you.

_____ 10. You can't look nice unless you wear expensive clothes.

_____ 11. You can always wear the same clothes for several days in a row.

_____ 12. Bleach is safe to use on all clothes.

_____ 13. Wear underwear and socks for a week, and then change.

_____ 14. When buying trendy clothes you will wear only once or twice, it's okay to buy items of lesser quality.

_____ 15. Clothes will wrinkle if you stuff the dryer too full.

_____ 16. A $16 shirt marked "dry clean only" is a better buy than a $20 cotton/polyester shirt that is washable.

_____ 17. Clothes made of wool or rayon usually need to be dry cleaned.

_____ 18. You should wear your dressiest party clothes to a job interview.

_____ 19. Clothes need washing if they look or smell dirty.

_____ 20. How you dress at work doesn't matter if you do your work.

Name_____ Date _____

This Is for Me!

Directions: Using a newspaper or magazine, find and cut out two or more styles of clothing that you feel would look good on you. Paste them in the space below. Then, write one or two sentences telling why each item would be flattering to you. Describe where you would wear the item. Add extra pages if necessary. (If you prefer, you may draw the clothing.)

Name_____ Date _____

This Is Not for Me!

Directions: Using a newspaper or magazine, find out and cut two or more styles of clothing that you feel would NOT look good on you. Paste them in the space below. Then, write one or two sentences telling why each item would not be flattering to you. Add extra pages if necessary. (If you prefer, you may draw the clothing.)

UNIT III
Getting Along with Others

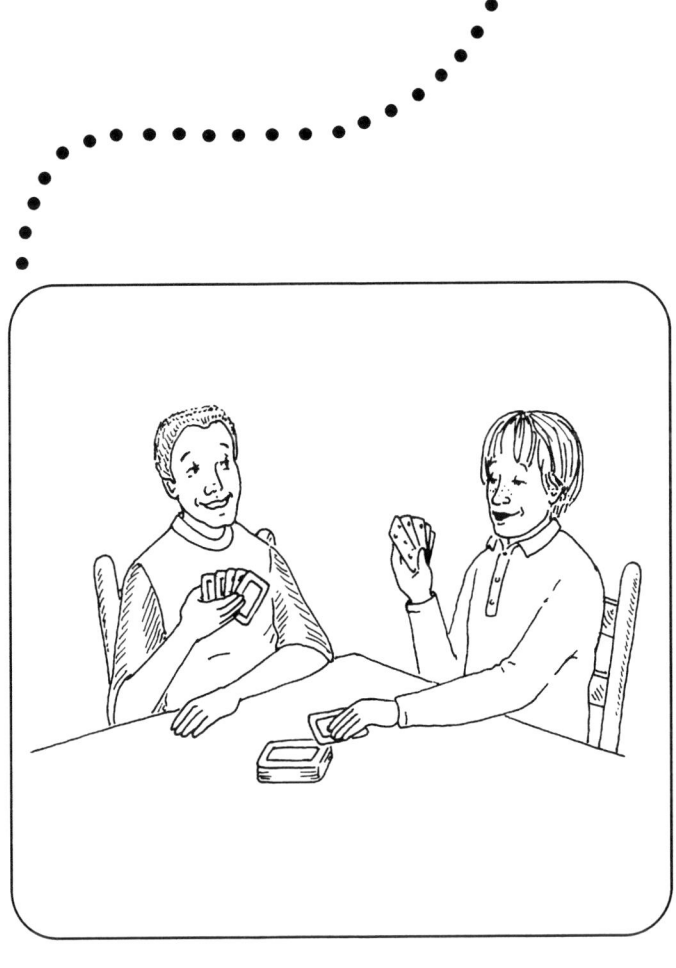

Getting Along with Others. . . . .

Objectives

Students will learn the meaning of friendship.
Students will learn the importance of getting along with others.
Students will learn how to be a friend to others.
Students will learn ways to be considerate of others.

Vocabulary

acquaintance	dignity	gossip	rumor
complaint	disagreeable	loyal	self-centered
considerate	embarrassed	quality	sexual harassment
criticize			

Additional Activities

1. Discuss characters in popular TV shows who act in a selfish manner.

2. Have students role-play the following situations. First, have them play the role selfishly. Then have them replay the situation in a way that is considerate of others.

    (a) One person fixes dinner while others sit around talking or watching TV.

    (b) People eat around a large table.

    (c) Someone comes in from outside with winter clothes on.

    (d) Two people are talking and a third person wants to join in.

    (e) One person bumps into another in the hall.

3. Divide students into pairs. Have each pair of students role-play a situation two ways: first showing selfish actions, and second showing considerate actions. Each pair of students should come up with their own skit.

4. As a class, make a list of ways one could build a friendship.

5. Discuss what a person could do to make friends in a new situation. For example, ask students how they would make friends at a new job or at a new school.

6. Have students role-play some situations that could present a problem in a relationship. Examples:

   (a) Your friend fails the math test. You get an A.

   (b) An acquaintance spreads the rumor that you cheated on a test.

   (c) A friend wants to copy your homework.

   (d) You plan to meet a friend for lunch. You get confused about the time and miss her. Now she's mad.

   (e) You told a friend about a problem you have. Now it's all over school.

   (f) You hurt a friend's feelings because you told him you didn't want to go bowling with him.

   (g) A co-worker becomes a pest, wanting all your attention all day and calling you at home.

   (h) A friend borrows your camera and doesn't return it.

   (i) A co-worker complains loudly about the boss to you.

   (j) A co-worker gets a poor job evaluation. He comes to you to complain about how unfair the boss is.

   (k) A friend is always late when you plan to do something together.

   (l) A friend smokes when he visits you. You don't want smoking in your home.

   (m) A co-worker asks you nosy questions.

   (n) You like a co-worker, but she loves to gossip about other workers.

   (o) You found out that a co-worker is always late to work. He or she sneaks in the side door and never gets caught. This seems unfair. You want to tell the boss.

   (p) A co-worker takes a two-hour lunch break every day and wants you to cover for her.

   (q) You borrowed $5 from a friend and forgot to pay him back until now—one month later.

(r) Your boss wears an out-of-date hairstyle. You think she'd look much prettier in a more modern style. You think you'd be doing her a big favor by telling her so.

(s) You hate your boss's strong perfume.

(t) You are invited to a party at a friend's home. Not realizing it is a dressy occasion, you show up in jeans.

(u) A co-worker keeps telling you dirty jokes. You don't enjoy this.

(v) Your boss tells you to do something, but you don't really understand what he means.

(w) You know that one of your co-workers drinks alcohol on the job.

7. Have students role-play the following situations between a worker and his or her boss. Or, the teacher may play the boss.

(a) Your boss tells you your work is sloppy. She thinks you are in too big of a hurry.

(b) Your boss criticizes you for being late to work for the third time in a week. You *were* late, but you know that two other people were too.

(c) Your boss feels your work area is messy.

(d) Your boss tells you to get a haircut.

(e) Your boss tells you your clothes are not appropriate for work.

(f) Your boss tells you that you may not smoke on the job.

(g) At the last minute, your boss asks you to work late. You have a dental appointment.

(h) Your boss wants you to go on a date with him or her. A pay raise is mentioned as a possible benefit.

(i) Your boss praises you for a job well done.

(j) Your boss invites you and some other workers to a party at his home.

(k) You find out it is your boss's birthday.

(l) You'd like to give your boss a holiday present, but can't spend much.

(m) Your boss gives you a small, but nice, present on your birthday.

(n) Your boss is not very friendly.

(o) Your boss wants you to help at his son's birthday party. You really don't want to, but are afraid to say no.

(p) Your boss asks you to do more work than another worker, who you know makes more money than you do.

(q) You can't make ends meet on your paycheck. You've been working for three years without a raise.

(r) Your boss asks you to do a job you know you can't handle.

(s) Your boss explains a task to you, but you don't understand what you are to do.

(t) Your boss's grooming is terrible. You know he would look better if he cleaned up.

(u) Your boss makes a mistake on your paycheck.

(v) You are the newest worker. Your boss seems to give you all the worst jobs.

(w) You get in trouble for something you didn't do. Your boss thinks you messed up the job, but it was actually someone else.

(x) Your boss acts as though he doesn't like you.

(y) Your boss is too friendly. He wants you to go out for drinks with him every night after work.

(z) Although she doesn't know it, you are in love with your boss (who is married).

8. Have students role play making a complaint. Have them follow the guidelines on page 42 for disagreeing without being disagreeable.

(a) Your brother borrows your pen without asking.

(b) Your sister borrows your shirt without asking and doesn't give it back.

(c) Your teacher tells the class there will be a major test on the same day as the class play. You wonder if she'd give the test on another day.

(d) A friend borrows your bike and damages it.

(e) A friend spreads stories about you behind your back.

(f) A friend says he can't go out with you because he is sick. Later, you find out that he went somewhere with another friend instead.

(g) A teacher marks your answer wrong. You think you should get credit for it.

(h) You tell a friend in confidence about your dad's drinking problem. Your friend tells other people.

(i) Your friend has terrible body odor.

(j) Your friend complains all the time. It really gets to be a drag.

(k) Your friend tries to monopolize you. This person wants you to spend all your time with her and won't let you have any other friends.

(l) One of your friends is always trying to tell you what to do.

(m) Your friend is planning a costume party. Everyone else thinks it is a dumb idea.

(n) Your friend always wants you to play tennis. You try it a few times but you don't enjoy the game.

Name_____ Date_____

Building Friendly Relationships

Getting along with others is one of the most important things you'll ever learn to do. Some people you know are your acquaintances. Others are your friends.

Acquaintances are people you know by name but do not know really well. At school, acquaintances may be other students you see and talk to in class. They may be members of the same club or sports team. You have things in common with your acquaintances. You like each other. But you don't spend a lot of time together or know each other that well.

On the job, most of your co-workers are probably acquaintances. You may eat lunch or take breaks together. One or more of your co-workers may become your friends. Most will probably remain acquaintances.

Friends are different from acquaintances. You know a friend much better. You see or talk to a friend often. You do things together. A true friend is someone special.

A friend is someone who likes you a lot. A friend likes to do the same things you like to do. A friend feels the way you do about a lot of things.

A true friend is loyal to you. A friend stands up for you and stands by you. A friend understands and accepts you the way you are. A friend respects you and is thoughtful of you. A friend enjoys spending time with you.

Everyone needs at least one good friend. And everyone needs a variety of acquaintances to make life fun and interesting.

••What Did You Learn?

1. How is a friend different from an acquaintance?

_____

_____

2. How do you think an acquaintance could become a friend?

_____

_____

Name_____ Date_____

Being a Friend to Others

In order to make friends, you need to be a friend to others. In other words, you need to act like a person *you'd* like to have for a friend.

Are you a good friend to others? To find out, rate yourself on the questions below. Write **U** (**Usually**), **S** (**Sometimes**), or **R** (**Rarely**) on the line in front of each question.

_____ 1. Do you act like yourself around others? After all, you want people to like the real you, not some fake image you try to keep up.

_____ 2. Do you listen when others talk? By listening, you make the other person feel special.

_____ 3. Are you loyal to your friends? No one can trust a person they know talks behind the backs of others. Don't repeat secrets someone has shared with you.

_____ 4. Are you understanding of others? If you judge others for their mistakes, they won't like it.

_____ 5. Are you considerate of other people's feelings? Try not to do anything to hurt or anger other people.

_____ 6. Do you treat others like they are important to you? Call them by name. Let them know you are interested in and respect them as people.

_____ 7. Do you run down other people? No one likes to be criticized. Try to accept others as they are.

_____ 8. Do you borrow other people's things? It's okay to do this once in awhile. But, don't ask all the time. And, pay back what you owe right away.

_____ 9. Are you unhappy a lot? No one wants to be around someone who complains all the time. Try to look on the bright side as much as possible.

_____ 10. Do you brag? No one wants to hear someone talk about how great they are all the time.

_____ 11. Do you tell others what to do? Most people don't like being bossed around.

Name_____ Date_____

What Do You Think?

1. Why do you think it is so important to be able to get along with others?

   _____

   _____

2. Why do you think it is better to be yourself rather than putting on an act?

   _____

   _____

3. What things do you think you can do to show others that they are important to you?

   _____

   _____

4. Why do you think it takes work to get along well with others?

   _____

   _____

5. What do you think are the most important qualities a friend should have?

   _____

   _____

6. What kinds of things do you think a good listener does?

   _____

   _____

7. Think of your own best friend. Name the three qualities you like most about this friend.

   _____

   _____

   _____

Name_____ Date_____

Being a Friend

Directions: In each box below, write **Yes** if you think the person is being a good friend. Write **No** if the person is not. Then tell why you wrote **Yes** or **No**.

1. "I don't think the boss likes Juan. I know why . . ." Is this speaker being a good friend to Juan? _____ Why or why not? _____ _____ _____ _____	4. "I did so well in the soccer game! Too bad you didn't get any goals." Is this speaker being a good friend? _____ Why or why not? _____ _____ _____ _____
2. "I'm sorry you lost your ring. I know it meant a lot to you." Is this speaker being a good friend? _____ Why or why not? _____ _____ _____ _____	5. "Al told me this in secret. I shouldn't tell, but . . ." Is this speaker being a good friend? _____ Why or why not? _____ _____ _____
3. "Way to go, Julia. I'm glad you got the job!" Is this speaker being a good friend to Julia? _____ Why or why not? _____ _____ _____ _____	6. "I promised to meet Vic at noon. It's 12:30. I'd better go." Is this speaker being a good friend to Vic? _____ Why or why not? _____ _____ _____ _____

Thinking of Others

Have you ever known anyone who acts like the people below? Have you ever done any of these things yourself?

- When Jacinta finishes making a snack, she leaves everything out on the counter.

- When Michael finishes his shower, he leaves the towel on the floor.

- Enrico turns the TV up so loud, no one in the house can stand it.

- Leah interrupts everyone. She just can't wait her turn to talk.

- Wang doesn't pay attention to where he is going and bumps into a woman carrying a baby.

- Jill loves to get gifts. But she doesn't remember anyone else's birthday.

- Montel sees no reason to say "please" or "thank you."

None of these people are being considerate of those around them. They are acting in a self-centered way. These people are thinking only about their own needs, wants, and interests. They are so busy thinking about themselves that they forget to think about others.

Self-centered people are often not fun to be around. Other people get tired of being around people who think only of themselves.

Try to act in a way that is considerate of others. Clean up after yourself. Do your share to help out around the house. Treat friends, family, and even strangers kindly. Be considerate of other's needs and possessions. Be polite to other people, even people you don't know.

If you treat others considerately, they will enjoy being with you. You will find it is easier to make and keep friends. And you'll have the satisfaction of knowing that you are a thoughtful and considerate person.

Name_____   Date_____

Doing the Considerate Thing

Directions: Write **C** by the actions below that are **considerate**. Write **S** by the actions that are **selfish**.

_____   1. Seeing your roommate carrying two large bags of groceries, you volunteer to help.

_____   2. You play the radio loudly in a crowded lunchroom.

_____   3. You tell people over and over about the vacation you are planning to take this summer.

_____   4. You mail a card to a friend in time for her birthday.

_____   5. Someone gives you a box of candy. You share it with your friends.

_____   6. There is a crowd waiting to buy tickets to a concert. You push to the head of the line.

_____   7. Seeing that the living room is a mess, you put things away without being asked.

_____   8. Your brother is watching television. You come into the room and change the channel.

_____   9. An aunt gives you a gift. You write a thank-you note.

_____   10. You whisper to a friend during an assembly.

_____   11. You hold the door open for an elderly woman.

_____   12. Because your parents are both very busy, you offer to make dinner for the family.

_____   13. You bump into someone in the hall. She drops her books. You say "excuse me" and help her pick them up.

_____   14. After taking a shower, you hang up your towel and put the soap in the soap dish.

_____   15. You start to hiccup in the library. You leave the room until the hiccups have stopped.

_____   16. Your friend gives you a great birthday gift. You never get around to thanking her for it.

How to Disagree Without Being Disagreeable

Making and keeping friends can be hard work. There are many times when you will not agree with another person. You may even be angry with him or her.

Learning how to disagree with someone without being disagreeable yourself is an important skill. There are times you will need to disagree with a friend, a parent, a teacher, or even your boss. Learning how to do so in the right way will prevent a lot of problems.

First of all, you should know that it is okay to stand up for yourself. If you disagree with something someone else does, you have a right to tell him or her. Don't make a fuss about small things. But, if it is important, speak up. You can learn to do this without being unkind or making an enemy of the person.

Here are the basics:

1. Speak calmly and firmly as you state your views. Don't get mad. Don't insult the other person.

2. Let the other person answer. Listen to what they have to say.

3. Try to solve the problem. Don't let the discussion wander onto another topic.

4. End the conversation on a friendly note.

Let's look at an example. One of your co-workers keeps borrowing lunch money from you. You're tired of this. You might say to her, "There's something I need to talk to you about. I'm tired of lending you lunch money so often. You owe me $15 in all now. I need to get it back."

Hopefully, the person will be embarrassed and pay back at least part of the money. If she refuses, you should stop lending her money.

In any case, you have stated the problem in a dignified way. If the other person gets mad or won't cooperate, he or she is not much of a friend. You might say that you're sorry to have this problem between you. This way, you've ended the conversation on a positive note.

         Learning Basic Social Skills

More Disagreements

Directions: Read each situation below. Write what you would say if you were faced with that problem. Follow the rules for disagreeing on page 42. There is more than one correct answer for each problem.

1. At work the person at the next desk plays her radio all day. It's too loud for you. You prefer to work in a quiet space. What do you do?

_____
_____
_____
_____
_____

4. Another student always talks to you while the teacher is talking. You wish he'd stop. What do you do?

_____
_____
_____
_____
_____

2. The student who sits next to you in math cracks her knuckles during tests. What do you do?

_____
_____
_____
_____
_____

5. You are sick and miss a week of work. Another worker spreads the rumor that you really went out of town. What do you do?

_____
_____
_____
_____
_____

3. Your co-worker gets a raise and a better job. You don't, but you sure wish you had! What do you say to your co-worker?

_____
_____
_____
_____

6. Another worker borrowed your favorite jacket. He hasn't returned it. What do you do?

_____
_____
_____
_____

Name_____ Date_____

Keeping a Good Relationship with Your Boss

There may be times when you have a disagreement with your boss (or teacher). In this case, you have to be very careful how you work out the problem.

• • When the boss criticizes your work

If your boss has a complaint about your work, listen! Apologize for the error. Say you'll do better next time. You've been hired to do the job right, after all!

• • When you have problems with other workers

Try to work out the problem on your own. If you can't handle the problem, ask the boss for help. But, be careful. It doesn't make you look good if you're always having problems with your co-workers.

• • If the boss gets too friendly

A boss who flirts or makes improper remarks to you is out of line. You should stand up for yourself. Tell him or her that you don't like what's going on. Ask your boss to stop. It is against the law for a boss to harass employees. (It's called sexual harassment.)

• • Your boss doesn't want to be friends.

Your boss isn't supposed to be your friend. Hopefully, you'll be on friendly terms. But you share a business relationship, not a friendship.

Directions: Getting along with your boss is important. What do you think are some of the best ways to do this?

_____

_____

_____

_____

_____

Problems on the Job

Directions: Read each problem below. Circle the letter of the answer that describes what you should do if you want to keep a good relationship with your boss. Give a reason for your choice.

1. Your boss corrects you for a mistake you made. You

   (a) get mad.

   (b) have hurt feelings.

   (c) try to blame someone else.

   (d) try to learn from what you've been told.

The reason for my answer is:

_____

_____

_____

2. Your boss gives an office party at his home. You

   (a) go and have a very good time getting loud and silly.

   (b) stay home; the party is not during working hours.

   (c) go and use your best manners.

   (d) stay home since you see the boss too much at work.

The reason for my answer is:

_____

_____

_____

3. You don't like your boss. You

   (a) tell other workers why you don't like him.

   (b) tell him what you don't like about him.

   (c) act like you like him.

   (d) ignore him as much as possible.

(continued)

Problems on the Job *(continued)*

The reason for my answer is:

_____

_____

_____

4. Your boss makes a mistake. You

    (a) tell everyone else about it.

    (b) keep quiet about it.

    (c) phone *his* boss and tell on him.

    (d) remind him of it when he corrects your mistakes.

The reason for my answer is:

_____

_____

_____

5. Your boss says your clothes aren't right for the job. You

    (a) don't wear them again.

    (b) tell her you'll wear whatever you want to.

    (c) tell her you just paid $50 for them.

    (d) tell her that her clothes aren't right either.

The reason for my answer is:

_____

_____

_____

More Problems on the Job

Directions: Read each problem below. Write what you would do to solve each problem. There is more than one correct response to each problem.

1. Your boss is always flirting with you. You don't feel comfortable at work anymore.

   _____

   _____

   _____

2. You forget a co-worker's name when you start to introduce her to a friend.

   _____

   _____

   _____

3. Your boss compliments you on your work in front of everyone. Some of the other workers tease you about being the favorite.

   _____

   _____

   _____

4. Your boss tells you that your work has not been good enough.

   _____

   _____

   _____

5. A co-worker asks you how much money you're making. You'd rather not tell her.

   _____

   _____

   _____

Name_____ Date_____

Unit Test

Directions: Write **True** or **False** on the line before each statement.

_____ 1. A friend should be loyal to you.

_____ 2. A friend listens to what you say.

_____ 3. A friend makes you feel good about yourself.

_____ 4. You should never tell a friend if he or she does something that bothers you.

_____ 5. Treat your boss just like your best friend.

_____ 6. Get mad when you disagree with someone. That way the other person will listen to you.

_____ 7. Acquaintances are people we know by name, but we don't know them very well.

_____ 8. Most people have more acquaintances than friends.

_____ 9. Friends and acquaintances are the same thing.

_____ 10. Gossiping may cost you friends.

_____ 11. It's never okay to borrow anything.

_____ 12. If you borrow, pay back as soon as possible.

_____ 13. Bragging is a good way to impress people.

_____ 14. Criticizing things lets people know you think things through.

_____ 15. Treat others as if they are special and important.

_____ 16. It's best to let the boss solve any problems that arise with your co-workers.

_____ 17. Getting along with others is important for a happy life.

_____ 18. Getting along with others often takes work.

_____ 19. All your co-workers will become your close friends.

_____ 20. You should always become close friends with your boss.

What Is a Friend?

Directions: Below are many qualities a person might have. Decide which of these qualities are important to you in a friend. Mark each quality **very important**, **sort of important,** or **not important.** Put an **X** in the box of your choice.

A good friend . . .	Very important	Sort of important	Not important
is good looking.			
has nice clothes.			
is honest with you.			
agrees with you on most things.			
is good in sports.			
likes you just the way you are.			
listens to you.			
makes you feel special.			
is loyal to you.			
helps you out if you need it.			
has plenty of money.			
likes the same things you do.			
gets good grades.			
is popular with others.			
makes you feel good about yourself.			
is thoughtful and considerate.			
is fun to be around.			
likes to spend time with you.			
has a good car.			

What Kind of Friend Am I?

Directions: Look at the qualities you marked "very important" on page 49. Think about which of these "very important" qualities describe yourself. Write a paragraph in the space below. Tell about your own strong points in being a friend to others. If there is an area in which you need to improve, tell about it in a second paragraph.

My strong points as a friend:

_____

_____

_____

_____

_____

_____

_____

How I could improve as a friend:

_____

_____

_____

_____

_____

_____

_____

Am I a Considerate Person?

Directions: How do you measure up? Are you usually considerate of others? Or, do you go about thinking mainly of yourself? Think about your actions as you answer each question below. After each question, write **Yes** or **No**.

1. Think about conversations you have with others:

   (a) Do you wait until others have finished speaking before you speak? _____

   (b) Do you talk about things of interest to others? _____

   (c) Do you talk about a variety of topics rather than the same thing over and over again? _____

2. Think about how you act in a public place:

   (a) Are you quiet at public meetings or concerts so that you don't disturb others? _____

   (b) Do you say "Excuse me" if you bump into someone? _____

   (c) Do you wait your turn quietly when standing in line? _____

3. Think about how you act at home:

   (a) Do you keep your things orderly and picked up? _____

   (b) Do you leave the bathroom neat and clean? _____

   (c) Do you clean up after yourself when you fix a snack or cook? _____

   (d) Do you offer to help with chores? _____

   (e) Do you respect the rights of other family members? _____

   (f) Do you remember the people you care about with a card or gift on their birthdays? _____

   (g) Would your family describe you as an easy person to live with? _____

UNIT IV
Developing Conversation Skills

UNIT IV
Developing Conversation Skills . . . .

Objectives

Students will learn how to introduce two people.

Students will learn what to say when introduced.

Students will learn good ways to start a conversation.

Students will learn types of questions to avoid in conversation.

Students will learn how to accept a compliment.

Students will learn how to apologize and how to accept an apology.

Students will learn ways to stand up for what he or she feels is right.

Vocabulary

accident	discussion	interrupt	rumor
apologize	dramatic	introduce	situation
argument	embarrass	introduction	stammer
compliment	exchange	personal	topic
conversation	gossip	positive	typist
criticism			

Additional Activities

1. Have students practice introducing people to each other. Provide a variety of name tags with names, ages and positions (if applicable) of people. Some sample name tags might be:

Ana, age 16	Bob, age 17
Mrs. Wilson, English teacher	Senator Jackson
your mother	your dad
your sister, Jean	Rev. Nguyen, minister
your aunt, Mrs. Ramirez	your friend, Joe

> your grandmother, Mrs. Young   Coach Sampson
> your school principal   your uncle, Mr. Gomez

You could have students think of more names to go on the tags. Then combine all the tags and have pairs of students draw two tags each. The students in each pair should then practice making introductions between the two people described on their name tags.

2. Use the same pairs of students as in Activity 1. Assign one of the students to begin a conversation with the second student. For example, the student playing "your grandmother" might start a conversation with "your friend Bob."

3. Assign one student to come to the front of the class to play the role of a person of a given age and sex. Let the other students try to come up with appropriate conversation starters they might use if meeting this person for the first time. Write the ideas on the board.

4. Have each student think of three social errors for which one would need to apologize. Have students write the errors on index cards (one to a card). Collect all the cards. Then distribute the cards randomly among the students. Have the students take turns acting out how they would apologize for each error. Another student may act as the injured party and respond correctly.

Some examples of social errors are:

(a) Spilling coffee on the couch at a party

(b) Breaking a lamp at a friend's house

(c) Forgetting to go to a dentist appointment

(d) Denting your friend's car

(e) Tearing your sister's blouse you borrowed

(f) Breaking your mom's vase

(g) Running over your sister's bicycle and ruining a wheel

(h) Forgetting to take out the garbage for your father

(i) Losing the spare set of car keys

(j) Hitting a ball through a neighbor's window

(k) Forgetting a lunch date with a friend

(l) Making a lot of errors on a letter you typed at work

(m) Forgetting to go to a meeting at work

(n) Arriving late at work due to oversleeping

(o) Accidentally hurting a friend's feelings

(p) Making a long personal phone call at work

(q) Staying at lunch too long, and getting caught by the boss

5. Divide the class into teams of two. One student can play a person who wants to say "no" to another person. The second person is trying to force the first person to do something. Some sample situations to role-play follow. Students may come up with more ideas. (Assume that "you" does not want to do whatever is involved.)

(a) Someone asks you to help him or her cheat on a test.

(b) Someone wants you to have a beer with them.

(c) Your friends have been drinking. You don't want to drive home with them.

(d) A stereo salesman tries to push you into buying *now*. You aren't ready to make a decision.

(e) A friend asks you to give money to a charity she's collecting for. You don't like that charity.

(f) Your boss wants you to work on Saturday. You've already made other plans that you can't change.

(g) A friend wants to borrow your car.

(h) Your friend's father is pushing you to eat seconds on dessert. You're trying to lose weight.

(i) Someone tries to give you a big helping of a food you don't like.

(j) Your date wants you to stay out past the time you should be home.

(k) Your friends decide to spray paint graffiti on the school.

(l) A friend pressures you to smoke a cigarette.

(m) Someone invites you to a party. When you arrive, everyone has been drinking.

(n) Your friends want to drag race.

(o) Someone asks you to be in charge of the spring dance.

(p) Your friends want to have a party at your house while your parents are out of town.

(q) Your friends think you should buy a dress you've tried on. You decide you can't afford it.

(r) All your friends are joining a protest march for a cause you don't believe in. They want you to join them.

(s) A friend wants you to come over. You're at home enjoying an old movie on TV.

(t) Your friends want you to go skating. You want to stay home and work on your car.

(u) Everyone at school is wearing popular brand-name shoes. You try them on, but they don't feel very comfortable. Your friends try to talk you into buying them anyway.

(v) Your teacher asks you to join a club at school. You really aren't interested.

(w) A friend asks you to be in charge of decorations at a party. You don't think that's your thing. You would rather help with the invitations.

(x) Your boss wants to know if you can finish a project by 3:00. You are sure you can't finish before 5:00.

6. Divide the class into pairs. Have each pair practice giving and receiving a compliment graciously. Some possible topics for compliments might include:

   (a) compliment on a piece of clothing the person is wearing

   (b) compliment on a recent achievement

   (c) compliment on a job well done

7. Have each student in the class design a poster illustrating one rule of conversation skills. Students should write the rule they are illustrating on the poster.

The Skill of Conversation

A conversation is like a game of catch. For it to work, both people must take part. Both must talk. Both must listen. A good conversation is an exchange of ideas and thoughts.

Have you ever tried talking to someone who talks so much you can't say anything? Or a person who has nothing to say? Both of these people need to improve their conversation skills.

When you are talking, look at the other person. Talk about things you think will interest the other person. Don't talk on and on. Give the other person a chance to answer you.

When the other person is talking, pay attention. Don't interrupt. Don't start talking while the other person is talking.

What can you talk about? One way to pick up things to talk about is to keep up with what's going on in the world. Read the paper. Listen to the news on TV. Read magazine articles. If you have a hobby, learn more about it. For example, if you like cars, read up on the latest models. This will give you something new and interesting to talk about.

Sporting events are a topic of interest to many people. You'll be able to add to the conversation if you know something about current events in sports.

There are other topics that you should not talk about. Here are a few of the no-no's:

- unkind remarks about other people

- rumors or gossip

- criticism of others

- too much talk about yourself

- your personal problems

- your medical problems

- bad language or dirty jokes

58
Learning Basic Social Skills

Making Introductions

Have you ever been in a situation like this? You are out shopping with your dad. As you round the corner of the fresh fruit display, you see the school principal, Mrs. Parks.

Your dad and Mrs. Parks have never met. So, you should introduce them. Do you know what to do? Or, do you hem and haw around until the two introduce themselves?

Many people are not sure of themselves when making introductions. But, you just need to remember two things:

Always say the name of the older or more important person first.

By saying an older person's name first, you show respect. Likewise, by saying an important person's name first, you show honor to that person.

If you are the person being introduced, you have some things to do too. Smile at the other person. Say "Hi" or "Hello." You may add, "How do you do?" or "I'm happy to meet you." Look the other person in the eyes. Shake hands if you wish. (This is a friendly thing to do.)

•• *Introduction Practice*

Circle the person in each pair below whose name should be said first in an introduction.

(a) your mom a school friend	(d) a senator your neighbor
(b) your sister a teacher	(e) a teenager an elderly man
(c) Dr. Williams your grandmother	(f) the mayor your friend

59   *Learning Basic Social Skills*

Allow Me to Introduce You

Directions: Write **Correct** or **Incorrect** on the line in front of each introduction below. If it is **Incorrect**, tell why.

_____ 1. "Clint, this is my mom."

_____

_____ 2. "Grandma, this is my friend Manuel."

_____

_____ 3. "Reverend Olsen, this is my uncle, Mr. Chatham."

_____

_____ 4. "Micah, this is my friend Barb."

_____

_____ 5. "Dad, I'd like you to meet Senator Ingram."

_____

_____ 6. "Coach Goldman, this is my brother Fred."

_____

_____ 7. "Dr. Robinson, this is my little sister Allyse."

_____

_____ 8. "Matthew, this is my boss, Mr. Gomez."

_____

_____ 9. "Mother, this is my new friend Anthony."

_____

_____ 10. "Erica, I'd like you to meet Bert Smith."

_____

Getting a Conversation Started

Once you've been introduced to someone, how do you start talking to this person you've just met?

•• *Good Conversation Starters*

One way to get the ball rolling is to give the other person a compliment. Here are some examples:

"Your sweater is beautiful. Is it handmade?"
"I hear you play football for Murrah High. That's a good team."
"So, you work for Habitat for Humanity. That's a great cause."

Another way to start a conversation is to ask the other person a general question. This should show that you are interested in knowing more about the person. Some examples are:

"Where do you go to school?"
"How long have you lived here?"
"Where do you work?"
"What do you think the Braves' chances are in the World Series?"

•• *Poor Conversation Starters*

Some questions are too personal. Don't ask questions that could embarrass or hurt the other person. Avoid questions about a person's private life. Most people don't like to be asked about money matters either. Here are some examples of questions that would NOT be good to ask:

"How much money do you make?"
"Don't you know it's not good for you to be overweight?"
"What is wrong with your leg?"
"You sure are short!"
"How can you afford that new sports car?"

What if someone you've just met asks you a question that is too personal or rude? Don't be rude back. Just say, "I'd rather not talk about that." Then change the subject.

What to Say After You Say Hello

Directions: Imagine you are at a party. You want to get a conversation going with a person you don't know. Write **Yes** by each question that would be a good conversation starter. Write **No** beside each question that is not.

_____ 1. "Do you think the weather will turn cold again?"

_____ 2. "Where do you go to school?"

_____ 3. "That's a nice shirt. How much did it cost?"

_____ 4. "What hobbies do you enjoy?"

_____ 5. "Why don't you do something about your weight?"

_____ 6. "What team are you for in the Super Bowl?"

_____ 7. "How long have you lived in Portland?"

_____ 8. "Isn't that girl's dress ugly?"

_____ 9. "Did you hear about my stomach operation?"

_____ 10. "Where do you work?"

_____ 11. "Have you heard the latest about Maria's boyfriend?"

_____ 12. "Do you like Mexican food?"

_____ 13. "How do you think the Lakers will do this season?"

_____ 14. "I like your outfit. That color is great on you."

_____ 15. "Don't you think you should have dressed up today?"

Directions: Imagine you are at a friend's house. He is not ready to go to the movies yet. You have to wait in the living room with your friend's dad. You have never met him before. Write two questions you could ask to start a friendly conversation.

1. _____

_____

2. _____

_____

Name_____ Date_____

The Conversation Game

Directions: Imagine you have just met each person below. Think of a question you might ask each one to start a conversation. Make sure your question will be of interest to that person. (There are many correct answers for each example.)

1. A 65-year-old retired teacher

   _____

2. A college soccer player

   _____

3. A 30-year-old car salesman

   _____

4. Your friend's grandfather

   _____

5. A school board member

   _____

6. A 21-year-old college student

   _____

7. A high school graduate now working as a waitress

   _____

8. A musician who is in a wheelchair

   _____

Rate the Conversation

Imagine that you are a new worker in a big company. You are in the lunch-room at work. A person whom you met once before sits down with you. You know this person only by name. But, you'd like to get to know him better. You wonder what to talk about.

Read each remark below. Decide if it would be good to use in conversation. After each remark, write **Yes** or **No**. Then explain why it would or would not be a good conversation starter.

1. "Who do you think will win the Super Bowl?"

   _____

2. "I hear that Molly in the accounting department is getting a divorce. Do you know why?"

   _____

3. "I'm just getting over a gall bladder operation. The doctors said it was amazing I lived. First, they made a four-inch cut. . . ."

   _____

4. "I hear that our lunch hour time will be changed. How do you think that will work out?"

   _____

5. "I'm the best typist in the office. I can type 80 words per minute."

   _____

6. "Mark is such a slow worker. I can do any job twice as fast as he can. I wonder what's wrong with him."

   _____

7. "My boss, Mr. Houston, isn't too smart. I don't think he knows what he's doing."

   _____

8. "I saw an interesting TV show on computers. Do you use one?"

   _____

9. "Did you hear there is a tornado warning out for tonight?"

   _____

Accepting a Compliment

Jamilla and Jeri are talking before class.

Jamilla: That's a great looking shirt!

Jeri (looking away and turning red): Oh, it's not that great! It's so old I can't believe I wore it today.

What do you do when someone gives you a compliment? Many people (like Jeri) get embarrassed. They don't know what to say. They may stammer and deny the compliment is true.

By doing this, you're really sort of putting down the person who gave you the compliment. Jeri may make Jamilla feel as though she doesn't have very good taste. Or, Jamilla may feel like she said the wrong thing.

It's better to accept compliments you are given. Say something like, "Thank you. It's very comfortable," or "Thank you. I got it for my birthday."

If someone compliments you on something you've done well, accept the compliment. Don't say, "It was nothing." Smile and say something like, "Thank you. I enjoyed working on that job."

Directions: Each person below is getting a compliment. Write a polite acceptance of each compliment.

1. You did a great job handling the cash register during rush hour today.

   _____

2. Your uniform looks sharp. With that attitude, you'll go far with my company!

   _____

3. You are my children's favorite baby-sitter. They always ask for you first when I need to get a sitter.

   _____

65 *Learning Basic Social Skills*

Name_____ Date_____

Making an Apology

Sometimes you may need to apologize for something you did wrong. Maybe you said something to hurt someone's feelings. Maybe you broke or damaged something belonging to another person. Do you know what to do?

The first thing to do is to go to the other person as soon as possible. Admit your mistake. Don't try to cover it up or hide it.

Then, say you are sorry. Do whatever you can to make up for the mistake.

Let's look at an example. Your boss asked you to make 20 copies of a chart he wants to pass out at a 3:00 meeting. You forget to do it. At 3:00, your boss is looking for the copies. What do you do?

1. Apologize.

2. Admit you forgot.

3. Make the copies right away and get them to the meeting.

Here's a second example. Another worker in your office has a favorite coffee mug. One day, you knock it off the counter and break it. She is out of town. No one else saw you do it. What do you do?

1. Apologize when she gets back.

2. Admit you broke the mug.

3. Replace it with another mug.

Directions: Each person below needs to apologize. Write a good apology in the space below.

1. You're an hour late to work. _____
_____

2. You made five mistakes typing this letter. _____
_____

3. You left a mess in the lunchroom. _____
_____

4. You lost my pen. _____
_____

Accepting an Apology

We've talked about making an apology. But, what if you are the one who has been wronged? You may be upset or angry at the other person. But, if the person apologizes, do your best to accept the apology in a nice way.

If you are on the receiving end of an apology, listen to the apology. Then accept the apology. Say something like, "I understand what happened," or "I know it was an accident." If the person offers to try to make good for the mistake, it is okay to let him or her do so.

Let's look at an example. Your friend borrows your watch. By accident, she breaks the band. She comes to you and apologizes. She explains what happened. Then she offers to have the band repaired.

You should accept the apology. Then you should say something like, "Thanks. It would be really nice of you to have it fixed for me."

Remember, accidents happen to everyone. It's best to repair the damage as quickly as possible and be done with it. This way, there are no hard feelings.

Directions: Each person below is offering an apology. Write a good answer accepting each apology.

1. I'm sorry I was late to pick you up. I had to stop and get gas.

   _____

   _____

2. You know the jacket you lent me? I spilled some coffee on it. I'd like to take it to the dry cleaners and have it cleaned for you. I'm so sorry.

   _____

   _____

3. I'm sorry I forgot your birthday. Here's your gift a day late!

   _____

   _____

Standing Up for Your Rights

There are times when you need to stand up for your rights and say "no" to another person. It is hard for many people to say "no." They are afraid of hurting the other person's feelings. They may be afraid the other person won't like them. But there are times everyone has to stand up for what they know is right.

Not long ago, there was a story in the paper about a group of high school students who drove to a party together. When it was time to go home, it became clear that the driver had been drinking. Most of the kids got in the car anyway. But one girl wouldn't go. She said, "No thanks. I'm going to call my dad to come get me."

The others made fun of her. But on the way home, the boy who had been drinking ran off the road. One teen was killed, and the others were injured.

Not all times you should say "no" will be as dramatic as this one. Saying "no" to a pushy salesman can save you money. Saying "no" to an unwanted job can save you time. In these cases, the important thing is that you have the right to control your own life. If you are always letting others talk you into doing things you don't want to do, you're not in control.

Of course, there are many times you can't say "no." When your mom asks you to take out the trash. When your teacher gives an assignment. When your boss gives you a job to do. In these cases, you must do as you are asked.

It is very different if you are asked to do something you feel is wrong. Or something you can't afford. Or something you don't enjoy. Or maybe something you just don't feel good about. In these cases, you'll be a lot happier by being your own person. These are times you should say "no."

How do you do it? It's not always easy. Be calm. Don't yell or argue. Don't put down the other person. Just make it clear that you're doing what you feel is right. Don't back down just because others try to force you.

This is more easily said than done. But you'll feel better about yourself in the long run for doing what is right.

It's Your Right to Say "No"

Directions: Imagine you are in each situation below. Someone is trying to get you to do something you do not want to do.

In one or two sentences, write how you could tell each person "no." Be polite but firm. Do not get rude or angry. Do not put down the other person.

Problem 1: You try on a shirt in a store. The salesman is pushing you to buy it. You don't really want the shirt. But the salesman won't give up. You say:

_____

_____

_____

Problem 2: At the last minute, your boss asks you to work overtime. You have already worked overtime two nights this week. And tonight you have a date you don't want to break. You say:

_____

_____

_____

Problem 3: The person you've been dating wants to see you every night. You like this person a lot. But you don't want to commit to every night. You say:

_____

_____

_____

Problem 4: A friend wants to borrow your car. You don't want to lend it. It's not new, but you've worked hard to pay for it. You know that your friend is sometimes careless.

_____

_____

_____

Name_____ Date_____

Discussion Skills

It may be just a friendly discussion about sports. Or, it may be a discussion at work about a problem that needs to be solved. But problems can arise when people need to discuss an issue. Here are a few pointers for making discussions go better:

1. Be willing to listen to other people's points of view. Hear them out. You may learn something.

2. If you disagree, be nice about it. You might say, "I don't agree with you about that," or "I feel differently about that."

3. State your opinions calmly. Don't lose your temper or shout. Be polite. Don't call the other person names or make fun of him or her.

4. Offer your own ideas. Make your suggestions in a positive way.

Good discussion skills are important. Practice the discussion skills listed above. You'll find you get along better with friends, family and co-workers.

Directions: Below are some people making suggestions with which you disagree. Reply to each statement. Tell why you disagree. Offer another idea. Be polite.

1. A co-worker says: "Let's buy the boss a box of candy for Valentine's Day." But you know the boss is trying to lose weight.

   _____

   _____

2. A group is discussing plans for a class party. You think you have some better ideas than those suggested so far.

   _____

   _____

3. A friend says: "Let's eat lunch at the new place on County Line Road." But you ate there once. The food was awful!

   _____

   _____

Unit Test

Directions: Put an **X** on the line beside the best way(s) to complete each sentence. There may be more than one right answer for each question.

1. The introductions below that are correct are:

   _____(a) "Charles, this is my mother."

   _____(b) "Aunt Betty, this is my friend Sally."

   _____(c) "Senator Jones, this is my brother José."

   _____(d) "Molly, this is my boss, Mrs. Wilson."

   _____(e) "Grandma, this is my friend Arthur Brown."

2. When you begin a conversation with someone you don't know, you should

   _____(a) ask about the person's private life so you can get to know them faster.

   _____(b) give the other person a compliment.

   _____(c) ask a general question like, "Where do you go to school?"

3. When you are talking to someone, you should

   _____(a) take turns talking.

   _____(b) look at the other person.

   _____(c) talk as much as possible.

   _____(d) pay attention to what the other person is saying.

   _____(e) interrupt only if you have something more important to say.

   _____(f) gossip only if the other person knows whom you're talking about.

   _____(g) talk about yourself as much as possible.

   _____(h) tell all about your personal problems.

   _____(i) avoid using bad words and telling dirty jokes.

   (continued)

Unit Test *(continued)*

4. When someone gives you a compliment, you should

    _____(a) say it's not true.

    _____(b) smile and say "Thank you."

    _____(c) turn red and look at your feet.

5. If you need to apologize for something you've done, you should

    _____(a) say you are sorry.

    _____(b) apologize as soon as possible after the mistake.

    _____(c) try to cover up or hide your mistake.

    _____(d) try to make up for your mistake.

    _____(e) admit your mistake.

6. If you are asked to do something you feel is wrong, you should

    _____(a) go along with the crowd anyway.

    _____(b) give everyone a lecture on why they are wrong.

    _____(c) say "no" politely but firmly.

7. When you are discussing an issue with someone, you should

    _____(a) let the other person know how dumb his point of view is.

    _____(b) control your temper.

    _____(c) state your opinion calmly and kindly.

    _____(d) laugh at the other person.

    _____(e) be pleasant and positive.

    _____(f) speak as loudly as possible.

       Learning Basic Social Skills

Name_____ Date_____

What Should I Say?

Directions: Read each sentence below. Decide how sure you are of what to say in each situation. Put an **X** in the box that tells how you would feel: very sure of what to say, pretty sure I know, or not too sure. There are no right or wrong answers. The chart will show you areas you need to learn more about.

	Very sure of what to say	Pretty sure I know	Not too sure
1. You must introduce two people who don't know each other.			
2. You are being introduced to someone you don't know.			
3. You want to start a conversation with someone you just met.			
4. You are talking to someone you don't know very well.			
5. Someone gives you a compliment.			
6. You need to apologize for a mistake you made.			
7. You are asked to do something you feel is wrong.			
8. You are having a disagreement with someone.			
9. You forget someone's name when you want to introduce him.			
10. You must introduce yourself to someone you don't know.			
11. Someone asks you a personal question you don't want to answer.			
12. Someone apologizes to you for breaking something of yours.			

Name_____ Date_____

At a Loss for Words

Directions: Write a paragraph in the space below. Describe a time when you faced a problem involving conversation skills. (It could involve a disagreement, an apology, an introduction, or an embarrassing moment in conversation.) Explain how you handled the problem. What would you do differently the next time?

_____

_____

_____

_____

_____

_____

_____

_____

Directions: Think of a person you like to talk to. Why do you think that person is easy to talk to? Write a paragraph giving your reasons.

_____

_____

_____

_____

_____

_____

_____

UNIT V
Having a Good Work Attitude

UNIT V
Having a Good Work Attitude . . . .

Objective

Students will learn what it means to have a good work attitude.
Students will learn why having a good work attitude is important.

Vocabulary

ability	disagreement	experienced	quality
attitude	employee	outlook	situation
cooperate	enthusiasm	override	succeed
dependable	error		

Additional Activities

1. Discuss why appearance and attitude are so important to employers that they have been found to outweigh quality of work in consideration for employment, especially for entry-level jobs.

2. Have students write a paragraph telling their strong points and weak points in their attitudes and appearance.

3. Have students draw cartoons portraying a good work attitude and a poor work attitude in the same situation at work. For example, an employee has been corrected by the supervisor. The cartoon would show one good attitude toward the correction and one poor attitude. The cartoons could be displayed on a bulletin board.

4. Have students role-play a variety of situations showing a good versus a poor work attitude. One student (or the teacher) can play the supervisor. Two other students can play the worker with a good attitude and the worker with a poor attitude. The "supervisor" would make the same statement to both workers, one at a time. The "workers" would then respond appropriately to the roles. Some examples are:

76

a. **Supervisor:** You are not following the delivery route correctly.
   Worker #1: Oh, what difference does it make?
   Worker #2: I'm sorry. What's the problem?

b. **Supervisor:** I want you to start sweeping the workroom floor every morning.
   Worker #1: What for? It doesn't need it every day.
   Worker #2: O.K. I'll do it.

c. **Supervisor:** You need to restack those boxes in order.

d. **Supervisor:** You need to work faster clearing the tables during the rush hour.

e. **Supervisor:** Do you understand how to do the job?

f. **Supervisor:** Your pay will be docked if you are late again.

g. **Supervisor:** The job is not finished until you have cleaned up the work area.

h. **Supervisor:** You are the slowest worker in the factory. Can't you speed it up a little?

i. **Supervisor:** Here's a faster way to count change.

j. **Supervisor:** I need you to come in 15 minutes earlier in the morning. You can leave 15 minutes earlier at night.

k. **Supervisor:** I want you to learn how to balance tires.

l. **Supervisor:** That shirt doesn't look too good for work.

5. Make a list of what the class feels are the most important ways a worker can show a good attitude.

6. Make a list of ways a worker can show a poor attitude.

7. Have students work in pairs to write short stories about a worker with a poor attitude. They may read the stories aloud to the class or act them out. Students should choose a worker in an occupation that interests them. Students could then write another story about a worker in that same field who has a good attitude.

8. Have students make posters showing how a person could have a good work attitude in school. The poster should explain how good work attitudes in school would translate into good work attitudes on the job.

9. Invite a person who works as an employment interviewer to speak to the class about things the company looks for when hiring employees for its entry-level positions.

Your Work Attitude Counts!

Imagine you are an employer. You interview people who want jobs with your company. Many, many people are looking for work. You talk to them. You read about their schooling and their work experience.

But how do you decide whom to hire? What things really make the difference between who gets the job and who does not? What helps a worker who has already been hired keep a job?

Many studies have been done to answer these questions. The answers may surprise you.

Employers listed three areas as being the most important to them when hiring new employees. In order of importance, these were:

- **A good appearance**

- **A good work attitude**

- **Work skills**

The area most important of all to employers was the person's appearance. A person who was badly groomed or wearing dirty clothes did not rate a second look. A person who is neat and clean gives the impression he or she will do careful work as well. It pays off to pay close attention to your looks in the world of work!

The second most important area to employers is a person's attitude. Employers want a worker who is dependable and honest. The worker should be on time. He or she should follow company rules.

The worker should do his or her best work and have it done on time. The worker can be counted on to do the work correctly and follow directions.

A good attitude means the worker wants to learn. He or she shows an interest in the job. Employers want their workers to cooperate both with them and with their fellow workers. The worker should have a pleasant outlook.

(continued)

Your Work Attitude Counts! *(continued)*

It is also important that a worker be able to accept the blame for errors made and try to correct them. The worker should always accept the help of the boss or more experienced workers when learning a new job.

The last important area is work skills. You might think that your ability to do the job would be the most important thing. But this is not always true.

Of course, you will probably need some skills to even be considered for the job. But it is your appearance and attitude that will help you get (and keep) the job.

A bad appearance or attitude can override your other skills. No employer wants a worker who is messy, who can't get along with anyone, or who is always late.

A good appearance and pleasant attitude will help you succeed in whatever you do. A poor attitude, sloppy dress, and bad grooming will hold you back from getting the things out of life that you work for. No matter how smart or talented you may be, bad attitudes and bad grooming will get in your way every time!

• • *What Did You Learn?*

1. Put an **X** on the line by the two things the study said were the most important to getting a job.

   _____ good work skills   _____ a good attitude   _____ a good appearance

2. What do you think are some of the most important ways a worker can show a good attitude toward the job?

   _____

   _____

3. Why do you think a company might hire a person with fewer work skills over another person with better work skills for an entry-level job?

   _____

4. What do you think are the most important ways to keep your appearance attractive?

   _____

Get Hired!

Carmel was applying for a job as a file clerk in a large automobile dealership. She had earned good grades in her business classes in high school. And, she had worked part time as a file clerk in another business.

Carmel arrived for her interview with dirty hair, a dress that was too tight and a big hole in her stockings. When she filled out her application, she didn't follow directions. Her finished application was messy and incomplete.

Mr. Knight did not hire Carmel. He knew she had the skills to do the job. But her attitude and appearance turned him off.

Renada was the next girl to apply. She had gotten average grades in her high school business courses. She had no experience as a file clerk.

Renada arrived for the interview looking good. She was dressed simply, but she was neat and clean. When she filled out her application, she asked questions about the parts she didn't understand. She did a neat job with no mistakes. She was polite and showed interest in learning the job.

Mr. Knight hired Renada that day. He knew she didn't have all the skills needed. But he knew she could learn on the job. Her skills would improve with time. Renada was hired because she had a good attitude and pleasant appearance.

•• *What Do You Think?*

1. What changes do you think Carmel needs to make before her next job interview?

   _____

   _____

   _____

2. How do you think a person with a poor attitude or poor grooming could improve?

   _____

   _____

   _____

You're the Boss

Directions: Pretend you are the boss of a small company. You hired three workers a few months ago. Now you can keep only one of them.

Read the worker ratings below. Answer the questions. Tell which worker you will keep. Tell which two workers you will fire. Give reasons for your answers.

1.

Worker Rating Sheet

Quality of work _____*good*_____

Appearance _____*good*_____

Gets along with others _____*poor*_____

Attitude toward work _____*poor*_____

I will _____
(fire, keep)

this worker because …

2.

Worker Rating Sheet

Quality of work _____*fair*_____

Appearance _____*fair*_____

Gets along with others _____*good*_____

Attitude toward work _____*good*_____

I will _____
(fire, keep)

this worker because …

3.

Worker Rating Sheet

Quality of work _____*good*_____

Appearance _____*poor*_____

Gets along with others _____*good*_____

Attitude toward work _____*poor*_____

I will _____
(fire, keep)

this worker because …

4. Which worker did you decide to keep? Why?

Name_____ Date_____

Looking at Your Attitudes

Directions: Write what you would do in each situation below. Be sure your answer shows a good attitude toward work and toward your co-workers.

1. If I don't do something right the first time, I . . .

   _____

2. When I make a mistake, I . . .

   _____

3. If my boss or teacher points out I have made a mistake, I . . .

   _____

4. If I don't know how to do a job, I . . .

   _____

5. If someone offers me help on a job, I . . .

   _____

6. If I have a job to do, I . . .

   _____

7. If I don't think I can do a job, I . . .

   _____

8. If a job is too hard for me to do alone, I . . .

   _____

       Learning Basic Social Skills

Your Attitude Is Showing

Directions: Below are statements made by a boss. Circle the letter of the best answer the worker might make. Choose the answer that shows a good attitude toward work.

The boss says . . .

A good answer might be . . .

1. From now on your lunch hour will be from 1:00 to 2:00 instead of 12:00 to 1:00.

    (a) I'll die of hunger.
    (b) That's a dumb idea.
    (c) O.K. I'll remember that.

2. I want you to learn how to drive the new forklift.

    (a) Fine. I'd like to drive the new forklift.
    (b) I like the old forklift better.
    (c) I'd rather not.

3. Go to the supply room and get four reams of paper, one box of paper clips, and seven rolls of tape.

    (a) I can't remember all that!
    (b) I'm too busy! Ask Joe.
    (c) Let me jot that down so I get it right.

4. You made a mistake in the delivery to Jones Store.

    (a) I'm sorry. Show me what I did wrong.
    (b) I did not! I know I did it right.
    (c) It was Sally's fault.

5. Here's a better way to sort those letters.

    (a) I like my own way better.
    (b) Thanks. That is a good idea.
    (c) I've done it the old way for two years.

6. I want you to fix those three toasters before 5:00.

    (a) You've got to be kidding.
    (b) I'll try. I'll start right now.
    (c) What if I can't?

7. We'll have a staff meeting at 7:00 A.M. sharp!

    (a) That's too early for me!
    (b) I'll be there!
    (c) I don't get here that early!

What Do You Do?

Directions: Read each problem below. Write what you think you should do in each situation. Be sure your answer shows a good work attitude.

1. Two workers are talking. You need to ask one of them a question. What do you do?

   _____

2. Your boss is wearing a dress that is not flattering. You think she should know that. What do you do?

   _____

3. You try to look your best at work. But one day your boss tells you that you wear too much perfume. And he says the dress you are wearing is too short. What do you do?

   _____

4. Your boss explains a job to you. Later, when you begin work, you still aren't sure if you are doing it right. What do you do?

   _____

5. You are late to work for the first time all year. Your boss catches you. She gives you a lecture about being on time. What do you do?

   _____

6. You promised the boss you would work late Friday night to help meet a deadline. But then the boy (or girl) you've been dying to meet calls and asks you out. What do you do?

   _____

7. The worker at the desk next to you chews gum loudly all day long. It drives you crazy. What should you do?

   _____

An Employee Rating Form

Directions: Complete the employee rating form below. Pretend that you are the boss. The person you are rating is you. Put an **X** in the box for always, sometimes or not often. Be fair and honest with yourself.

If you now have a job, think about how you rate on each item at work. If you are in school and do not have a job, think of school as your job.

Item	Rating		
1. Quality of work	Always	Sometimes	Not often
(a) Work is neat	❑	❑	❑
(b) Work is done correctly	❑	❑	❑
(c) Work is done on time	❑	❑	❑
(d) Follows directions	❑	❑	❑
(e) Does best work	❑	❑	❑
Comments about the overall quality of this employee's work:			
2. Employee's appearance	Always	Sometimes	Not often
(a) Is well-groomed	❑	❑	❑
(b) Clothing is proper for the job	❑	❑	❑
(c) Clothing is neat and clean	❑	❑	❑
Comments about the overall appearance of this employee:			
3. Gets along with others	Always	Sometimes	Not often
(a) Cooperates with supervisor	❑	❑	❑
(b) Gets along with co-workers	❑	❑	❑
(c) Polite and well-mannered	❑	❑	❑
(d) Dependable and honest	❑	❑	❑
Comments about the overall ability of the employee to get along with others:			

(continued)

       Learning Basic Social Skills

An Employee Rating Form *(continued)*

Item	Rating		
4. Communication skills	Always	Sometimes	Not often
(a) Accepts correction well	❏	❏	❏
(b) Handles mistakes; accepts blame	❏	❏	❏
(c) Handles disagreements well	❏	❏	❏
(d) Speaks pleasantly to others	❏	❏	❏
Comments about employee's overall communications skills:			
5. Attitude toward work	Always	Sometimes	Not often
(a) Willing to learn new jobs	❏	❏	❏
(b) Shows interest and enthusiasm	❏	❏	❏
(c) Completes work without being told	❏	❏	❏
(d) On time to work	❏	❏	❏
(e) Follows company rules	❏	❏	❏
(f) Takes care of equipment and supplies	❏	❏	❏
(g) Cleans up after self	❏	❏	❏
(h) Makes good use of time	❏	❏	❏
Comments about employee's overall attitude toward work:			

What overall rating would you give this employee?

❏ Good   ❏ Fair   ❏ Poor

Which areas do you feel are the employee's strong points?

How might this employee improve?

Check the box that tells how you feel about this employee:

  ❏ I think we should keep this employee.

  ❏ I think we should fire this employee.

  ❏ I think we should give this employee three months to improve.
     If no improvement is seen, the employee will be fired.

Name_____ Date_____

Unit Test

Directions: The people below have job interviews with XYZ Company. Put an **X** by each thing that a person did that would be helpful in getting the job.

_____ 1. Marcus learned a little about XYZ Company's work ahead of time, so he could ask good questions.

_____ 2. Nina allowed extra time to get to her interview so she wouldn't be late.

_____ 3. Tania stretched the truth on her application to make herself look good.

_____ 4. Liz spent extra time on her appearance, making sure she was neat and clean.

_____ 5. Corey filled out the application the way she wanted to, not paying attention to the directions.

_____ 6. Jaime was pleasant and upbeat during his interview.

_____ 7. Maria got mad when the interviewer said she'd made a mistake on her application.

_____ 8. Tal said that he did not know how to do the work required, but that he was excited about learning how.

_____ 9. Rico said that he knew how to do the work even though he didn't.

_____ 10. Greg said he had a junior college degree. He didn't, but he thought no one would find out differently.

_____ 11. Sarita came to the interview straight from her workout. She explained that she was very busy and didn't have time to shower and change.

_____ 12. Reese needed a haircut. But he didn't take time to get one before the interview.

_____ 13. Kamal made a lot of mistakes on his application. He didn't want to ask questions about filling it out.

_____ 14. Matt knew he was a good worker. So, he didn't worry about his appearance in getting ready for the interview.

_____ 15. Katina smiled and acted interested when the interviewer explained the job she would do if hired.

Name_____ Date_____

How Does Your Work Attitude Rate? (Part One)

Directions: Read each sentence below. Put an **X** in the box that tells about your work attitudes.

	Usually	Sometimes	Not usually
1. I clean up after myself.			
2. I follow school/work rules.			
3. I try to be on time.			
4. I try to do my best work.			
5. I like to learn new things.			
6. I try to follow directions.			
7. I am polite to friends and teachers.			
8. I get along with teachers (or my boss).			
9. I try to look my best.			
10. People can depend on me to do the job.			
11. If I make a mistake, I admit it.			
12. I try to correct my mistakes pleasantly.			
13. I take care of my things.			
14. I am neat and clean.			
15. I ask for help if I don't know how to do something.			
16. I thank others for their help.			
17. I am honest and keep my promises.			
18. I keep at it when I have a job to do.			

Name_____ Date_____

How Does Your Work Attitude Rate? (Part Two)

Look back at the checklist you filled out on page 88. What are your strong points in your work attitude? In what areas do you think you could improve? Write your answers below.

The strongest points in my work attitude are:

_____

_____

_____

_____

_____

_____

_____

_____

I could improve my work attitude in the following areas:

_____

_____

_____

_____

_____

_____

_____

_____

Answer Key •••••••••••••••••••••••••••••••

Unit I: Looking Your Best

Student page 4: The Importance of Good Grooming

1. A person who is well-groomed is more likely to be a careful, neat worker than someone who is dirty and sloppy. Good grooming shows pride in oneself and a positive outlook. Good grooming is also a positive reflection on the company.
2. Poor grooming shows a low opinion of oneself. It shows a careless or inattentive attitude.

Student page 5: Clean Up Your Act!

1. soap and water
2. Deodorants control odor. Antiperspirants control wetness and odor.
3. Only soap and water can remove dirt and odors.
4. underwear and socks

Student page 7: Your Crowning Glory

1. A good stylist can help you choose a flattering hairstyle and products that will help your hair look its best.
2. Try a variety of products and see which one makes your hair look its best.

Student page 8: Be Handy with Hand Care

1. Use a nailbrush.
2. Clipping can cause rough edges or infection.
3. nail file, emery board, and nail clippers
4. Gently push them back with a towel after you wash your hands.

Student page 9: Face the Facts

1. a fluoride toothpaste
2. Floss removes food particles that the brush can't reach.
3. Visit the dentist regularly to take care of any problems that arise before they get out of hand.

4. A department store or pharmacy makeup counter
5. At least twice a day

Student page 11:   A Grooming Timetable

Answers will vary. Discuss the timetable as a group. Accept reasonable variations. If an answer is way off, discuss it further.

Student page 12: Unit Test

1. shower or bath
2. soap
3. deodorants
4. shampoo
5. emery board
6. dentist
7. trimming
8. fluoride
9. floss
10. appearance
11. Answers will vary. People react more positively to someone who is neat and clean. A person with body odor, dirty hair, bad breath, and so on, will turn others off. Such a person may have trouble on the job and in friendships.
12. Answers will vary. When you know you look your best, it makes you feel good. You know others are seeing you at your best. You know you are making a good impression.

Unit II: Choosing and Caring for Clothes

Student page 22: Choosing Easy-Care Clothing

Answers will vary:

1. This is a good choice because it should wear well and will look good. A reason not to buy is: it may shrink, and it will probably require ironing.
2. This is a good choice because it will wash well and should not need ironing. A reason not to buy is: André may prefer the look and "feel" of all cotton.
3. This is a good choice only because André likes it. A reason not to buy is: cleaning will be expensive.

Student page 24:   The Dryer Ate My Shirt!

Put an X by: 1, 2, 3, 4, 5

Put an X by: 8, 13, 15

Student page 26:   I Don't Have a Thing to Wear!

Answers will vary:

1. Answers will differ according to the norms of your community. Slacks or clean jeans without holes and a nice shirt might be appropriate.
2. Jamara should wear a conservative dress or skirt and blouse. She may wear a little makeup, but should avoid looking overdone.
3. Sue should wear a dressy dress or suit. Pants would not be appropriate. Omar should wear a suit or sports coat and slacks.
4. Kent should wear a suit and tie. If he does not own a suit, he could wear conservative slacks and dress shirt and tie. These should not be brightly colored or wildly patterned. He should look dignified and respectful.
5. If possible, Rita should observe what the other employees in the office are wearing when she goes in for her interview, and then dress similarly. If this is not possible, a conservative dress or skirt and blouse would be a safe choice for the first day.
6. Juan should dress neatly in slacks, a dress shirt, and tie. He could wear a suit, but this is probably not necessary in this situation. Jeans or shorts would be too casual for a job interview.

Student page 27:   How Would You Know?

1. The blouse or shirt should appear to be well constructed. There should be no loose threads or buttons. The material should feel strong. A polyester/cotton blend will require no ironing.
2. Check your appearance from head to toe, preferably in a full-length mirror.
3. Call the person who sent the invitation and ask what he or she will be wearing.
4. Look the coat over carefully. Are the seams wide and well sewn? Are the buttons sewn on securely? Does the material feel sturdy, or is it flimsy? Do plaids and patterns match at the seams? Is the hem sewn neatly without loose threads?
5. Underwear and socks should be worn only one day. Other clothing should be checked to see if it is dirty, bad smelling, or wrinkled before it is worn a second time.
6. Try on the clothing and look in a mirror in good light. Compare various colors and styles to see which looks best on you. Ask the opinion of a friend or a salesclerk (who may not give an unbiased response).

Student page 28: Unit Test

1. True. This is a good way to find out your boss's preference.

2. True. If you are buying an item that will be worn a lot, make sure it is of good quality because you will be washing it often.

3. True. Mixing and matching makes a limited amount of clothing go much farther.

4. True. The item should be taken to the cleaners.

5. True. Clothing made of polyester and cotton blends should come out of the dryer wrinkle-free if the dryer is not too hot or overloaded, and if the clothes are removed as soon as or before the dryer stops.

6. False. Work clothes should be clean, but they should also be of appropriate style.

7. False. For most job interviews jeans are too casual. Men should dress up in a suit or slacks, and women should wear a basic dress or skirt and blouse.

8. True. Some clothes of 100 percent cotton are preshrunk. They should not shrink when washed. If a 100 percent cotton item is not preshrunk, it may shrink when washed, especially if washed in hot water, then dried in a hot dryer.

9. True. People often judge others by their appearance.

10. False. You'll look nice if you buy clothes in styles and colors that flatter you.

11. False. You need to check to see if the clothes look and smell good before you wear them again. Underwear and socks should be changed daily.

12. False. Bleach may cause colors to fade. Read the directions on the label before using bleach. Do not use chlorine bleach on colored clothes.

13. False. Underwear and socks should be changed daily.

14. True. You won't need to get a lot of wear from such clothes, so you can buy an item that is more cheaply made.

15. True. If the clothes cannot tumble freely in the dryer, they will come out looking wrinkled.

16. False. It will cost $2 or more each time it is cleaned. So, it will soon cost more than the shirt that cost more to buy.

17. True. These fabrics will nearly always require dry cleaning.

18. False. Party clothes are not appropriate for an interview. Men should wear a suit or slacks, a dress shirt, and a tie. Women should wear a conservative dress or skirt and blouse.

19. True. You should never wear smelly or dirty clothes.

20. False. Research has shown that a person's appearance is very important in getting and keeping a job.

Unit III: Getting Along with Others

Student page 36: Building Friendly Relationships

1. You know a friend better than an acquaintance. It is a much closer relationship.
2. You would need to spend more time getting to know each other.

Student page 37: Being a Friend to Others

Answers will vary. Desirable answers are "usually" by #1, 2, 3, 4, 5, 6, and "rarely" by #7, 8, 9, 10, and 11.

Student page 38: What Do You Think?

Answers will vary. Suggested answers are:

1. A person who can't get along with others will have trouble making friends and getting along on the job.
2. You want people to like you the way you really are. If you put on an act, you won't be attracting people with whom you have the most in common.
3. You can show others that they're important by listening to them, showing an interest in their concerns, being considerate, etc.
4. It takes work because you must give your friends time and attention.
5. A friend should be understanding, kind, loyal, trustworthy, respectful, accepting, considerate, good company, etc.
6. A good listener pays close attention to what's being said, does not fidget or look distracted, does not interrupt, shows genuine interest in what the other person is saying, makes appropriate responses, etc.
7. Answers will vary.

Student page 39: Being a Friend

1. No. A good friend does not talk behind a friend's back. Also, a friend should not run down the other person.
2. Yes. A friend should be understanding in times of loss or trouble.
3. Yes. A friend should celebrate a friend's successes and show pride in the friend's accomplishments.
4. No. A friend does not brag about himself or put down the other person.
5. No. A friend doesn't repeat confidences.
6. No. A friend doesn't keep the other person waiting.

Student Page 41: Doing the Considerate Thing

1. c	5. c	9. c	13. c
2. s	6. s	10. s	14. c
3. s	7. c	11. c	15. c
4. c	8. s	12. c	16. s

Student page 43: More Disagreements

Answers will vary:

1. Go to the other person at a time when just the two of you can talk. Explain calmly that the radio bothers you. Say that you can't concentrate with it playing. Try to come to a solution. Perhaps she can turn it down or play it only part of the day. Thank her for her willingness to cooperate.

2. Go to the other person in private. Explain that the noise is bothering you. Ask her to please stop.

3. You should rise above your bad feelings and congratulate your co-worker for getting the raise.

4. Talk to the other student in private. Explain that you'd rather he didn't talk to you while the teacher is talking. Ask him to wait until after class, so you can give him your full attention.

5. Tell the person you are not happy that he or she is spreading rumors about you. Ask them to stop.

6. Remind the person that he hasn't returned the jacket. Say that you would like it returned.

Student page 44: Keeping a Good Relationship with Your Boss

Answers will vary. Suggested ideas are:

Keep a friendly but businesslike relationship.

Do your work correctly and on time.

Come to work looking clean and well-groomed.

Have a good work attitude.

Accept criticism in good spirit and learn from it.

Student page 45: Problems on the Job

1. (d) It is the job of the boss to make sure work is done correctly. Accept the correction pleasantly and try to do better next time.

2. (c) At an office party, think "office" more than "party." This is a time to show good manners and impress the boss. It is not the time to get wild and crazy; you'll regret it later.

3. (c) If you don't like your boss, it is still to your advantage to get along well with him or her. Be pleasant and friendly. Never talk behind his or her back.

4. (b) Being loyal to the boss is your best bet. Talking behind his back or trying to get him in trouble could cost you your job.

5. (a) You should dress as the boss wishes you to.

Student page 47: More Problems on the Job

1. Tell the boss you don't feel comfortable with such remarks. Ask the boss to stop.

2. Apologize and admit your faulty memory. (Example: "I'm sorry but I'm drawing a blank on your name.") Get the introduction over quickly and go on to something else.

3. Thank the boss for the compliment. Ignore or laugh off the teasing. (Be sure to avoid acting like you're better than the other workers.)

4. Apologize. Ask what you can do to improve. Follow through on trying to make the improvements suggested. Do not argue or get mad if your work is criticized.

5. Don't feel like you have to tell this information. Just say something like, "I'd rather not say." Then change the subject.

Student page 48: Unit Test

1. true	6. false	11. false	16. false
2. true	7. true	12. true	17. true
3. true	8. true	13. false	18. true
4. false	9. false	14. false	19. false
5. false	10. true	15. true	20. false

Unit IV: Developing Conversation Skills

Student page 59: Making Introductions

The following names should be circled:

(a) your mom
(b) your sister
(c) your grandmother
(d) a senator
(e) an elderly man
(f) the mayor

Student page 60: Allow Me to Introduce You

1. Incorrect. The woman's name should be first.

2. Correct. The older person's name should be said before the younger person's name.

3. Correct. The minister should be shown respect by mentioning his name first.

4. Incorrect. The girl's name should be said first.

5. Incorrect. The senator holds an important position, and therefore should be mentioned first.

6. Correct. The older person's name is said first.

7. Correct. The older person's name is said first.

8. Incorrect. The boss should be mentioned first, as he is older and is also an important person (to you).

9. Correct. Mention the woman's name first.

10. Correct. The girl's name is first.

Student page 62: What to Say After You Say Hello

1. yes	5. no	9. no	13. yes
2. yes	6. yes	10. yes	14. yes
3. no	7. yes	11. no	15. no
4. yes	8. no	12. yes	

Answers will vary. Suggested ideas are:

Compliment him on the house, yard, etc.

Ask a question related to sports.

Tell him why you enjoy being friends with his son.

Student page 63: The Conversation Game

Answers will vary. Be sure each question is appropriate for the person in the description. Be sure each question is in good taste and is not too personal.

Student page 64: Rate the Conversation

1. Yes. Nearly everyone has an opinion on this. Many people are very interested in this topic.

2. No. This is gossip.

3. No. No one wants to hear about it, especially over lunch.

4. Yes. Everyone will have an opinion about this!

5. No. This is bragging.

6. No. You don't make yourself look good by putting someone else down. You just look unkind.

7. No. It's not smart to criticize the boss, especially at work. Your words may find their way back to him.

8. Yes. Many people are interested in computers.

9. Yes. This is certainly a topic of general interest.

Student page 65: Accepting a Compliment

Answers will vary. The person should thank the person who gave the compliment. The person should not deny the compliment or argue with the person giving the compliment. Some suggested answers are:

1. Thanks. It sure kept me hopping!

2. Thank you. I like to look my best.

3. Thanks. They are great kids, and I enjoy baby-sitting them.

Student page 66: *Making an Apology*

Answers will vary. Each apology should contain a phrase saying the person is sorry. The person should admit the mistake and not try to cover it up or blame someone else. The person should not make excuses. If possible, the person should offer to make things right. Some suggested answers are:

1. I'm sorry. It won't happen again.

2. I'm sorry. I'll type it over right now.

3. I'm sorry. I'll go clean it up right away.

4. I'm sorry. I will replace it with a new pen.

Student page 67: *Accepting an Apology*

Answers will vary. Some suggested answers are:

1. That's O.K. We wouldn't get far on an empty tank. May I give you a dollar or two toward the gas?

2. All right. I would appreciate you having it cleaned for me.

3. Thanks! It was great of you to remember me!

Student page 69: *It's Your Right to Say "No"*

Answers will vary. Some suggested answers are:

Problem 1: No, thank you. I really don't want the shirt after all.

Problem 2: I'm sorry. I made some other plans for tonight. Would it be O.K. if I help out another night?

Problem 3: No. I like you very much, but I'm not ready for this yet.

Problem 4: No. I never lend my car to anyone.

Student page 70: *Discussion Skills*

Answers will vary. Some suggested answers are:

1. It's a great idea to remember her, but I know she's trying hard to lose weight. What if we give her flowers?

2. I've got a few ideas we might think about.

3. That place has great atmosphere, but I ate there last week and I didn't like the food. What if we try another restaurant instead?

Student page 71: *Unit Test*

Put an X by:

1. b, c, e	3. a, b, d, i	5. a, b, d, e	7. b, c, e
2. b, c	4. b	6. c	

Unit V: Having a Good Work Attitude

Student page 79: Your Work Attitude Counts!

1. Put an X by: a good appearance and a good attitude.
2. Answers will vary. A worker can show interest in the job, cooperate, have a pleasant attitude, be dependable, be on time, etc.
3. A person can be trained to do the work. It is more difficult to retrain someone with a bad attitude or poor appearance.
4. Answers will vary. Being neat and clean is most important. Wearing suitable clothes, etc.

Student page 80: Get Hired!

1. She needs to be sure she has showered and washed her hair. She should wear appropriate clothes. She should take her time with the application and ask questions about parts she doesn't understand.
2. Hard work over time.

Student page 81: You're the Boss

Answers will vary:

1. This worker would probably be fired because of a poor attitude toward work and an inability to get along with others. This worker is not that pleasant to have around.
2. This worker would probably keep the job. The quality of work is only average, but the worker gets along with others well and has a good attitude toward work. The boss could train the worker to improve in any skill areas that are lacking. This employee is good to have around.
3. This worker would probably be fired. The work is well done and the worker gets along with others. But a poor personal appearance and a poor attitude toward work would not make this worker very popular with the boss.
4. The best choice is worker #2.

Student page 82: Looking at Your Attitudes

Answers will vary. Suggested answers are:

1. Try to get it right the next time.
2. Admit it and try to make it right.
3. Ask how I can do better, and try to do it right.
4. Ask for help, and then listen to the directions.
5. Accept it thankfully and try to learn.
6. Keep at it until I have finished.
7. Ask someone for help so I'm sure I have it right.

8. Ask for help. Thank the person who helps.

Student page 83: *Your Attitude Is Showing*

1. c   2. a   3. c   4. a   5. b   6. b   7. b

Student page 84: *What Do You Do?*

Answers will vary. Suggested answers are:

1. Ask the question later if possible. If it is urgent, you might say something like, "Excuse me, just a minute. I needed to ask you about . . ."
2. You should do nothing. Keep your opinions to yourself.
3. Apologize. Stop wearing the perfume, or use just a little. Stop wearing that dress to work unless you can let the hem down.
4. Ask the boss or another more experienced worker about whatever you aren't sure about. This way you'll be sure to do the job correctly.
5. Apologize for being late. Don't make excuses. Say you'll try not to let it happen again.
6. You already promised the boss you would work. Try to set another time for the date. Explain the reason. Say that you'd really like to do it another time.
7. Ask them politely to tone it down.

Student page 85: *An Employee Rating Form*

These two pages should be completed at the same time. Answers will vary. The class should discuss the rating forms after they are completed. The teacher should examine the rating forms to see in which areas students feel they need more work.

Student page 87: *Unit Test*

Put an X by: 1, 2, 4, 6, 8, 15

Share Your Bright Ideas with Us!

We want to hear from you! Your valuable comments and suggestions will help us meet your current and future classroom needs.

Your name_____Date_____

School name_____Phone_____

School address_____

Grade level taught_____Subject area(s) taught_____Average class size_____

Where did you purchase this publication?_____

Was your salesperson knowledgeable about this product?   Yes_____   No_____

What monies were used to purchase this product?

____School supplemental budget   ____Federal/state funding   ____Personal

Please "grade" this Walch publication according to the following criteria:

Quality of service you received when purchasing ....A   B   C   D   F
Ease of use...A   B   C   D   F
Quality of content..A   B   C   D   F
Page layout ....A   B   C   D   F
Organization of material ....A   B   C   D   F
Suitability for grade level ....A   B   C   D   F
Instructional value...A   B   C   D   F

COMMENTS:_____

_____

What specific supplemental materials would help you meet your current—or future—instructional needs?

_____

Have you used other Walch publications? If so, which ones?_____

May we use your comments in upcoming communications?   ____Yes   ____No

Please **FAX** this completed form to **207-772-3105**, or mail it to:

Product Development, J.Weston Walch, Publisher, P.O. Box 658, Portland, ME 04104-0658

We will send you a **FREE GIFT** as our way of thanking you for your feedback. **THANK YOU!**